Communities of Activism

Communities of Activism

Black women, higher education
and the politics of representation

Edited by Jan Etienne

Trentham
Books
is an imprint of

IOE Press

First published in 2020 by the UCL Institute of Education Press, University College London, 20 Bedford Way, London WC1H 0AL

www.ucl-ioe-press.com

British Library Cataloguing in Publication Data:
A catalogue record for this publication is available from the British Library

ISBNs
978-1-85856-900-0 (paperback)
978-1-85856-916-1 (PDF eBook)
978-1-85856-917-8 (ePub eBook)
978-1-85856-918-5 (Kindle eBook)

Every effort has been made to trace copyright holders and to obtain their permission for the use of copyright material. The publisher apologizes for any errors or omissions and would be grateful if notified of any corrections that should be incorporated in future reprints or editions of this book.

The opinions expressed in this publication are those of the authors and do not necessarily reflect the views of the UCL Institute of Education, University College London.

Typeset by Quadrant Infotech (India) Pvt Ltd
Printed by CPI Group (UK) Ltd, Croydon, CR0 4YY
Cover design by emc design ltd, using images © Bella West/Alamy Stock Vector (woman) and Aaron Amat/Alamy Stock Vector (man)

Contents

About the contributors

Jan Etienne

Jan Etienne is Chair of the Womanism, Activism and Higher Education Research Network at Birkbeck University of London where she gained her PhD. She is a graduate of the School for Policy Studies, University of Bristol and teaches on Birkbeck's Education, Power and Social Change programme. She is the convener of the Education Globalisation and Change module and also co-chair of the Decolonising the Curriculum Working Group. Her major research interest is in the area of Black Feminist Epistemology and Womanist learning for community activism exploring black women's involvement in transforming community spaces into thriving matriarchal learning hubs. She was made a Birkbeck Fellow in 2019. Jan is author of *Learning in Womanist Ways: Narratives of first-generation African Caribbean women* (London: Trentham Books, 2016).

Ezimma Chigbo

Ezimma Chigbo is an undergraduate, youth practitioner and founder of The Luna Project, an organization that uses drama, music and creative writing to help young people understand themselves. She was elected Black Members' Officer for her student union. She has written and published articles on young women and street culture for online media outlets such as Black Ballad, and charity blogs within the youth sector. A youth worker and facilitator, Ezimma specializes in working with young women and people linked to street culture to explore issues including identity, violence, relationships and mental health.

Patricia Daley

Patricia Daley is Professor of the Human Geography of Africa at Jesus College, Oxford. She has taught a range of human geography topics, as well as specialist courses on African societies and environments. Her current voluntary work includes membership of the Council of the British Institute in Eastern Africa and of the Independent Advisory Group on Country Information of the Independent Chief Inspector of Border and Immigration. She is also a committee member and the equalities officer for the Oxford Branch of the University College Union. She chairs Fahamu Trust Ltd, a pan-African social justice movement building organization.

Jen Davis

Jen Davis works in Parliament and is a law graduate and currently completing a Master's degree in politics. She is creator and co-host of 'Consensus Podcast', a platform that discusses current affairs and politics from the viewpoints of black women. She is a member of the Diverse Communities Advisory Board, which advises the Shadow Secretary of State for Women and Equalities on issues faced by minorities. She is actively involved in politics and particularly youth and community activism. She works with young people on criminal justice and raising awareness of sickle cell disease.

Fyna Dowe

Fyna Dowe is an activist, vocalist, lyricist, writer and teacher. She is a multi-faceted creative performance poet and director of Head Healers Theatre Company. She has taught on a wide range of business, media and communications skills courses, developing and delivering entrepreneurial and mentoring skills to young adults. She is a motivator and communication skills expert, and has worked on college diversity programmes, leading high-profile women's development seminars, uplifting and inspiring women across various teaching and learning areas. She is co-founder and member of Lioness Chant, and has performed dub poetry to diverse audiences across the UK and abroad.

Patricia Gilbert

Patricia Gilbert commenced her PhD research in 2017 and is investigating the role of personal tutoring in contributing to the success of black and minority ethnic students and students from lower socio-economic backgrounds. Her background includes the co-ordination of an access to higher education programme and she was part of a small teaching team awarded the Times Higher Education 'Widening Participation Initiative of the Year' for a collaborative project with children's centres. Along with a variety of administrative roles in non-governmental organizations, she has taught in adult, further and higher education, and is currently an associate lecturer at Birkbeck, University of London.

Lurraine Jones

Lurraine Jones is a senior lecturer and Higher Education Academy Teaching Fellow in the Department of Psychosocial studies at the University of East London. She has been working on black British identities and cultures, and has conducted research into mixed-heritage identity and black British women. Her PhD thesis engages with the various dynamics of diversity training and how it impacts on black youth. She has extensive research experience working alongside diversity trainers in the Metropolitan police service.

Dawn Joseph

Dawn Joseph returned to higher education as an adult learner and gained her undergraduate degree in social sciences in 2015. She recently completed a Post Graduate Certificate in Criminology. She has a deep interest in criminology and until recently worked for the Centre for Justice Innovation, an organization committed to reforming the justice system through research, policy and practice development. Her office managerial role involved responsibility for overseeing the day-to-day operations of the centre, including managing relationships and contributing to its research. She is interested in research exploring levels of custodial sentencing in respect to black youth.

Nombuso Mathibela

Nombuso Mathibela is a writer, and activist interested in African feminist practice and Pan-Africanism. She graduated with a BA (LLB) from the University of Cape Town. In her final year she focused on critical legal studies, looking at the predicaments in legal education, pedagogy and the epistemic structural violence embedded in competition law. She held a Fellowship at the Tshisimani Centre for Activist Education and is working as an independent researcher and part of a popular education collective called *Pathways to Free Education,* which grew out of the education struggles in South Africa. Her primary areas of interest include black feminist philosophy, African feminist thought and the debates around law and decolonization. She is an activist researcher and is passionate about political education for the purposes of strengthening student movements in South Africa.

Uvanney Maylor

Uvanney Maylor is Professor of Education at the University of Bedfordshire. Her research interests include race, ethnicity, culture, educational equity, inclusion and social justice. She is particularly concerned about the impact of race and culture on educational practice/leadership and student and teacher experience, identities and outcomes. Prior to joining the University of Bedfordshire, she was a reader in education at the Institute for Policy Studies in Education at London Metropolitan University, and Director of

Multiverse (a professional resource network for initial teacher education). She also has a range of experiences working in activism with black communities in the voluntary sector in areas such as education, policing, crime, and minority ethnic health.

Palmela Witter

Palmela Witter works for Positive Futures Fund and has worked in various settings across the private, public and voluntary sectors. She has over 20 years' experience working within local authorities, schools and youth service as a manager and a voluntary sector chair and trustee. Her interest and passion in the research of children and young people, mental health and the survival of African Caribbean voluntary and community organizations led to her undertaking further higher education studies, where she recently graduated with an MSc in voluntary and community sector studies.

Cecile Wright

Cecile Wright works at the University of Nottingham as an honorary academic and independent researcher. She previously worked as Professor of Sociology at Nottingham Trent University. Cecile was the first black female professor in the East Midlands. She specializes in the areas of education, youth, social mobility and social exclusion. She was recently engaged by the Nottinghamshire Police and Crime Commissioner to investigate the relationship between the black and minority ethnic community and the police. Her expertise is wide-ranging and includes: education, health inequality, lifestyle, children and youth, family, welfare, women's interests, race relations, social class divide, community cohesion, politics and representation, crime and policing, and American civil rights.

Acknowledgements and editor's note

In working to put this volume together I owe a debt of gratitude to my fellow contributors and the many other women who walked alongside me and gave me strength and reason to continue believing in the power of solidarity, collaboration and sisterhood. Black lives matter and our personal testimonies break the silences that hamper our progress as we strive to promote the social and academic dimensions to higher education and learning. I give particular thanks to the invaluable support of the following colleagues and friends, without whom the inspiration for and completion of this book would not have been possible: Gillian Klein, Linda Milbourne, Yasmeen Narayan, Ursula Murray, Gail Lewis, Elizabeth Charles, Deborah Shallow, Marlene Benjamin, Judith McCleary, Yvonne Murray, Margaret George, Iesha Denize LaDeatte, Amber Fletcher, Patsy Cummings, Samantha Williams, Pauline Stephenson, Michele Beute, Carmelita Kadeena, Agatha Modeste, Megumi Waters.

And finally, I thank my husband Lloyd Gardner for his love and understanding and my brother, Stuart Etienne for his patience and forbearance.

~~~~~~~~~

This book about *Communities of Activism* was completed just before the shock onslaught of the devastatating Covid-19 (Coronavirus disease) pandemic, rapidly killing and impacting lives across the globe.

The world has changed dramatically.

In the midst of it all, we have no idea how society will recover from this deadly disease. Can we activists, whether in higher education or not, imagine a future after Coronavirus? One thing is certain: community activists of whatever type or political persuasion should be united and resolute in our efforts to confront the enormous challenges that lie ahead.

Jan Etienne, April 2020

Part One

Activism inside the academy

1

Chapter 1

Introduction. Education for survival: Black lives and black women's activism

Jan Etienne

Black women in higher education are bringing new energy to activist work. We feel liberated as we come together to reclaim our sisterhood now that black people and black youth in particular, are under siege. Our energy comes from a united and determined effort to withdraw from agonizing over discrimination and take charge of our destiny as we demand a new conversation on black lives and black academic success. As black women we reject the derisory measures we are often offered, disguised as significant steps towards progress. Such measures include the forums that inappropriately speak in our name and ignore our contributions when they are most needed. Activist sisters, both black and white, are collaborating with us and confronting the demons of structural racism that haunt every aspect of our social, economic and educational lives and impede our work in inspiring a new generation. In fostering a Womanist approach to education and learning we are resolute in our pursuit of new opportunities for collaboration.

Mirza and Gunaratnam (2014: 3) assert that:

> Black women activists have long drawn on their collective social and cultural knowledge to form strategic spaces of radical opposition and struggle for new forms of gendered citizenship in their communities. Coalitions have been, and continue to be, vital for black British feminist activism to thrive.

As black women in the various activist roles and educational spaces we occupy, we have never felt a more urgent pressure to represent. In this volume we share experiences of pain and suffering – of invisibility – but also of solidarity, challenge and success. We reveal the strategies that have enriched our lives as we find ways to support one another and have our say on initiatives to empower our community. Our desire for separate spaces of thought where we recover ourselves (hooks, 1990), is more relevant than ever as we confront the manifestations of whiteness that threatens to block our escape from the abyss that consumes us.

Black lives: Facing up to crisis

In today's climate of austerity and uncertainty in the fallout from chaotic Brexit politics, much still impacts negatively and disproportionately on black youth in the UK. Increasing numbers are permanently excluded from schools (DfE, 2018) and overrepresented in pupil referral units. In later chapters we discuss our approaches to pursuing change and our need to respond to a growing crisis of neglected black youth. In 2016/17 black children were permanently excluded from school at nearly three times the rate of white British pupils. Why, after decades of exposing the problem, are we still no nearer to finding solutions to this growing crisis? The Lammy Review (2017) into the treatment of black and minority individuals in the criminal justice system found that more than half the young people imprisoned in England and Wales were from black and minority ethnic backgrounds. And in 2018, of the 285 people stabbed to death, one in four were men aged 18–24, of whom a quarter were black. To add to this, black students are statistically less likely to achieve a higher-level degree compared to their white counterparts (Advance HE, 2019). Berry and Loke (2011) found that belonging to a minority ethnic community generated a statistically significant and negative effect on degree attainment. We deplore the failure of the services provided by public bodies to react appropriately, but we also question our own strategies for finding solutions. Increasingly we turn to higher education to assist in broadening our conversations and our understanding of the root causes of our concerns, and to work with others to effect change. For some of us in our later years, higher education may be seen as a possible means of galvanizing our lived experiences in the struggle to find justice in a climate of hate. In 2016 Birkbeck, University of London recruited 488 black women over the age of 50 (BBC Radio 4, 2016) on degree courses (the largest increase in three years) and alongside our studies we are increasingly joining together in activism with younger black women studying part-time at university. In the search for social justice, is higher education considered a social imperative for black women?

Inside the academy, however, key structures directly affect our own working lives. Although present, we are largely invisible in senior management (fewer than 1 per cent of professors are black) and we experience significant micro-aggressions (Gabriel and Tate, 2017; Rollock, 2012) in various forms. In 2017, Sian examined the effects of the structural and systemic nature of racism on black staff and found multiple micro-aggressions. Despite our own struggles in higher education, we seek a way forward and condemn the neo-liberal government policies that have failed us in wider society. A culture of cuts, contracts and competition across government services such as schools, health and social housing impact on all communities, but most severely on black lives. In particular, a once-thriving black voluntary sector established to deal with the shortfalls in mainstream government services is virtually disappearing as resources are cut (Milbourne and Murray, 2017). The sector can no longer play a key role in providing culturally sensitive services to black communities in important areas of social policy.

This book shares experiences of older and younger black women activists in higher education as we join other black activists in the community to play a vital role in a struggle to improve black lives. Our activism is manifested in many forms, including: intergenerational forums; our activist research roles; provision of extracurricular support and coaching; and our prose, chant, blogs, testimonies and discussions across social media. We acknowledge the transformative power of education and the important social dimension to learning.

What might a young black undergraduate female student, youth worker and survivor of a gang-related stabbing have to say about the relationship with knife crime and drill music? How does a senior lecturer in higher education and mother of four comprehend race awareness training and police relations with black youth? What does a young black female graduate, formerly excluded from school, creator of an online media platform tell us about her desire to receive coaching and remain focused on her goals? What drives a postgraduate black activist to return to learning aged 50, in order to work with other black women to revive the activities of the black voluntary sector? And what can a young South African activist researcher tell us about the forces that seek to supress our voice and our activism?

In challenging the sociologically framed black single mother narrative as normative (Reynolds, 1997), we also acknowledge the enormous societal pressures placed on the black man confronting a racist society. We reflect on educational strategies to improve black lives from our perspectives, views that are often silenced just when we urgently need solutions to tackling catastrophic problems, not least the escalating crisis of knife crime among black youth.

Our methodological approach

The chapters in this book bring together our professional experience in higher education research, teaching and community activist work. Many of us adopt a narrative study approach when analysing our oral and reflective accounts (Etienne, 2016). Additional empirical data is drawn from small-scale qualitative studies exploring black women's perspectives on black youth, crime and violence. And while our voices in the UK dominate these pages, we also explore important international, scholarly and activist dimensions.

How the chapters are organized

The book begins by mapping out major social concerns currently in the headlines that disproportionately impact Britain's black communities, and is constructed in three parts across three themes as follows:

PART 1: Activism Inside The Academy

The theme of Part 1 is the determination of black women to speak about their activism from inside the academy.

Chapter 1: Introduction

Jan Etienne outlines the key concerns and considers the influence of black women in higher education (as academics, students, researchers and alumnae) and their response to such challenges. The chapter makes a case for collective voices and black women's conversations to be heard in the light of a growing crisis.

Chapter 2

Patricia Daley confronts the challenges she faces and identifies how black women in the academy can promote learning for activism. She notes how community activism rests on the acceptance that a common, collective responsibility by black female academics is vital when there are so few of us. She proposes that academic labour, particularly for a black woman who is interested in social justice, is itself a form of resistance. The chapter maintains that the struggles of black people within the academy have come to the fore in UK universities, through local and national faculty and student campaigns exposing the discriminatory and exclusionary practices that stifle creativity, hinder our participation in knowledge production, block professional progression and legitimate white supremacy.

Daley seeks to break down the binary between the academic and the activist, especially when the academic is interested in curriculum diversity, supporting student movements and progressive change for the black community.

CHAPTER 3

Patricia Gilbert focuses on educational attainment and recounts her own educational journey in the UK education system in an effort to understand the educational experiences of black youth today. She investigates the attainment gap in higher education from a gendered, racialized and classed position, and engages with her experiences as a black woman involved in widening participation and in teaching in higher education. Gilbert points to the continuing gaps in the attainment of black students and those from lower socio-economic backgrounds, statistically less likely to achieve a 'good' degree (upper-second or first-class) than their more advantaged peers. The chapter concludes by considering calls to decolonize the curriculum and the potential that a more inclusive curriculum might have to 'transform educational institutions' and mitigate against the inequalities of outcomes faced by black students today.

CHAPTER 4

Cecile Wright considers the negative treatment of black female academics, illustrating how it operates and how activism is stifled. She describes her work as an activist and academic who gives voice to the otherwise voiceless. Such work focuses on black youth in Britain and their struggles in education. The chapter illustrates the Womanist mantra 'the personal is political' (Hill Collins, 1990) and recognizes the extent to which black women academics are inextricably linked to their communities (hooks, 1989, 1990). Her experience covers over three decades of research and scholarship in the field, in which she not only calls out and resists the negative hegemony of Britain's black community, but also illuminates the black community's ways of being that inspire healing and transformation.

PART 2: *Intergenerational Voices: Black Women Respond to Crisis and Black Youth*

This section explores our concern for black youth across a range of areas such as: knife crime, drill music, the police service and the British education system. The chapters adopt an intergenerational approach, as black women in education across the generations relate stories of challenge and resistance.

We hear from a cross-section of black women who are undergraduates and postgraduates working in areas such as the voluntary (third) sector, youth service and higher education, as they grapple with their influence in improving the lives of black youth. What is going wrong for black youth in the UK? Are we playing effective roles in their lives?

CHAPTER 5

Palmela Witter tackles the tragedy of knife crime in Britain's cities, where the bulk of victims are young black men. She stresses the urgency of bringing black women together to push for change in a fast-depleting black voluntary sector. She calls for collective action from black women in this volatile period.

How can black voluntary sector activists find creative strategies to investigate and tackle increasing knife crime among black youth? She reflects on the devastating tragedies we see as 'black on black' youth crime rises. She believes the time is right for black women activists in the voluntary community sector to create new platforms for change.

CHAPTER 6

This chapter considers drill music and its association with crime and violence.

Together, in conversations and reflections, Jan Etienne and Ezimma Chigbo seek to understand the anger and frustration behind the lyrics arising from the struggles of drill music creators. In a fast-moving social media world where the enticing world of drill draws a huge following, undergraduate student and youth worker Ezimma draws on her role as a young blogger to confront the issues in this male-dominated arena. She reflects on her blogs on drill music and exposes the 'normalization' of knife crime through drill by exploring the extent to which her own experience as a survivor of youth violence is reconciled. What can we learn about the racialized elements of the drill conversation in exploring the policing nature of drill narratives? Why is the issue of violent lyrics the major concern rather than an attempt to understand the poverty and struggles behind the genre from which the drillers preach?

CHAPTER 7

Lurraine Jones writes about the dynamics of police diversity training post-Macpherson. She considers the historical legacy of 'race' equality training in the Metropolitan Police service from the point of view of a black mother, higher education teacher and researcher. Engaging with a range of commentators, Jones problematizes the concept of 'race' and 'diversity' in the police services' recruitment and training programmes. She seeks to understand the interactions between the police and black youth and is determined not to underestimate the role of training in helping to improve relations. She asks: what do we know about the nature of pain and suffering of the black mother when confronted with evidence of police brutality and their negative interactions with black youth?

CHAPTER 8

Through interview and case study reflections, Jan Etienne and Dawn Joseph analyse the value of transnational education and the black male child. After completing a bachelor's degree, Dawn Joseph, a mother and graduate returns to higher education at the age 50 to undertake a diploma in criminology. The chapter discusses her experiences of 'successful mothering' as a single parent. She recalls the type of strategies she employed that resulted in a positive educational experience for her son in the British education system. What influence did the earlier years living in the Caribbean have on her son's educational success? What were the challenges faced, and what factors aided her success? Her story begins with a letter to her son as he approaches his 29th birthday.

PART 3: *Black Women in Higher Education, Supporting and Collaborating Internationally for Change*

Part three examines our key concerns and the approaches we deem necessary for inspiring and achieving success. The three chapters in this section provide insights from an international and UK perspective. What is missing from our knowledge and from our curriculums? What should we know so that we might deliver and reap the fruits of our activism? What can we learn from a younger generation? In an effort to avoid restating the painful narratives, how can we mobilize radically in collaboration with all our colleagues to effect change? And how can we pass on culturally sensitive knowledge and inspire the next generation? As black women, we ask: how important are discussions of critical black consciousness (raised in earlier chapters) in the British university curriculum?

CHAPTER 9

Activist scholar Nombuso Mathibela offers an international perspective on challenges to our activism. She uses a South African activist model to show how activist work is often silenced in our quest for social justice. She spotlights the historical marginalization of black women activists and the silencing of their activist voices as a lesson to black women across the African diaspora. Through the South African case study of disappearance she shows how black women's political representation and their insistence on total subjectivity and agency has come out of a collective desire to recognize the importance of black women activists' experiences. These black women fought against marginalization in national liberation movements and black consciousness movements. Despite their concealment in popular history, their connections to black women's history of knowing across the African diaspora is vital and contributes to the collective history of black women's activism. Their struggle and stories must not be silenced but should appear in education curriculums across the globe.

CHAPTER 10

In this intergenerational chapter Jan Etienne, Jen Davis and Fyna Dowe consider 'Whiteness' and its impact on black learners in higher education. We do this from the perspectives of black multi-faceted activists, educators, mentors and entrepreneurs. We recognize that black students of African heritage are among the fastest growing ethnic groups entering university and are the largest ethnic minority population. How can we support the university, motivate ourselves and learners in a climate where strategies are increasingly being adopted in higher education by British universities to decolonize university curriculums – strategies that are still fiercely criticized by the largely white power elite? As black women we speak of our strategies for achieving academic success and energizing black students to evolve from successful achievers to black academic role models. We can only do this with the support of our colleagues. Ultimately, we are pursuing 'collaborative activism' against 'whiteness' but accept that to fight inequality we first have to convince those who benefit from the 'invisible hand' to recognize their privilege. How might this be possible in higher education?

CHAPTER 11

Uvanney Maylor looks at the support given to black students by black women over and above their mainstream responsibilities and how this can help activism to flourish. She seeks to expose some of the challenges faced by black female students and academics in higher education and show how such difficulties can be used to promote community activism. As a black woman academic who previously worked in the community sector, she helps black female students at master's and doctoral level to overcome the challenges that threaten to undermine their commitment to succeed. Black women face questions about their abilities when white academics fail to understand their choice to study black focused topics or those with race as a central dimension, which may be deemed not academic or worthy of study. Maylor uses black feminist themes and theories associated with an ethic of care to engage black community activism in areas of health, education and politics. She reveals resistance and survival skills that have been developed to support black women as they navigate higher education. The chapter shows the strategies we find to support activism from inside the academy on behalf of black students, going beyond the call of duty to benefit our wider community.

Chapter 12

In the final chapter, Jan Etienne reflects on the themes raised in the book and suggests a way forward for black women in higher education who are engaged in activist work with sisters in the community. She reiterates the critical issues impacting black youth and prioritizes action on education and learning, including measures to supplement important initiatives to decolonize the university. She stresses the urgent need for ongoing coaching conversations with expert black contributors to be part of the university learning curriculum, in an effort to deliver a greater, appropriately enlightened university curriculum that inspires black learners and gives them a clear focus. Such an initiative has the potential to inspire confidence, produce higher attainment levels and increased success, ultimately benefiting the black student, the university and all those who participate in it.

References

Advance HE (2019) 'Degree attainment gaps'. Online. https://tinyurl.com/ycbqb7yt (accessed 7 December 2019).

BBC Radio 4 (2016) 'Returning to education over 50'. *Woman's Hour*, 26 August. Online. www.bbc.co.uk/programmes/b07pd4yw (accessed 11 December 2019).

Berry, J. and Loke, G. (2011) *Improving the Degree Attainment of Black and Minority Ethnic Students*. York: Higher Education Academy.

DfE (Department for Education) (2018) 'Ethnicity facts and figures: Education, skills and training: Pupil exclusions'. Online. https://tinyurl.com/srd4ft2 (accessed 7 December 2019).

Etienne, J. (2016) *Learning in Womanist Ways: Narratives of first-generation African Caribbean women*. London: Trentham Books.

Gabriel, D. and Tate, S.A. (eds) (2017) *Inside the Ivory Tower: Narratives of women of colour surviving and thriving in British academia*. London: Trentham Books.

Hill Collins, P. (1990) *Black Feminist Thought: Knowledge, consciousness, and the politics of empowerment*. Boston: Unwin Hyman.

hooks, b. (1989) *Talking Back: Thinking feminist, thinking black*. London: Sheba Feminist Publishers.

hooks, b. (1990) 'Choosing the margin as a space of radical openness'. In hooks, b. *Yearning: Race, Gender, and Cultural Politics*. Toronto: Between the Lines.

Lammy, D. (2017) *The Lammy Review: An independent review into the treatment of, and outcomes for, black, Asian and minority ethnic individuals in the criminal justice system*. London: Lammy Review. Online. https://tinyurl.com/yyctz8zf (accessed 9 December 2019).

Milbourne, L. and Murray, U. (eds) (2017) *Civil Society Organizations in Turbulent Times: A gilded web?* London: Trentham Books.

Mirza, H.S. and Gunaratnam, Y. (2014) '"The branch on which I sit": Reflections on black British feminism'. *Feminist Review*, 108, 125–33.

Reynolds, T. (1997) '(Mis)representing the black (super)woman'. In Mirza, H.S. (ed.) *Black British Feminism: A reader*. London: Routledge, 97–112.

Rollock, N. (2012) 'Unspoken rules of engagement: Navigating racial micro-aggressions in the academic terrain'. *International Journal of Qualitative Studies in Education*, 25 (5), 517–32.

Sian, K. (2017) 'Being black in a white world: Understanding racism in British universities'. *Papeles del CEIC: International Journal on Collective Identity Research*, 2, Article 176, 1–26. Online. https://tinyurl.com/qrd7w67 (accessed 5 December 2019).

Black women academics: Politics of representation and community activism in the African diaspora

Patricia Daley

This chapter discusses the potential role that black women academics in the UK can play in promoting learning for community activism. Helping to tackle critical issues faced by black communities and the African diaspora involves the histories of racism, exclusion and marginalization endured by black people in the UK and the global North. This means that those in the academy can play a critical role in providing the intellectual tools to raise consciousness, build solidarity and facilitate empowerment for emancipation. To be effective in such an endeavour would require the acceptance of a collective responsibility among black women academics. This may be difficult in view of how few there are within higher education institutions. This chapter argues that the increasing presence of black women in the academy opens up discussions of the interconnections between scholarship and community activism.

Since 2014, the struggles of black people within the academy have come to the fore in UK universities through local and national faculty and student campaigns, notably Black British Academics, Black Doctoral Network, 'Rhodes Must Fall' (Chantiluke *et al.*, 2018), and 'Why is My Curriculum White?' These mobilizations for academic freedom expose the discriminatory and exclusionary practices in UK universities that stifle creativity, hinder effective participation in knowledge production, block professional progression, and legitimize white supremacy in academic spaces designated as scientifically objective and politically neutral. While these black-directed campus struggles existed in pockets in the 1970s, they can now reach national and global attention through social media.

Until the 21st century many black intellectuals who were interested in social justice occupied peripheral positions in the UK academy. If they had the good fortune to be employed in a university they tended to find common cause with Marxists or socialist groups (such as sociologist and cultural theorist Stuart Hall). Racism meant that UK black intellectuals operated largely outside the academy in public activism, lending their support to community groups and protest movements. So, we are at a pivotal moment in terms of the space black people occupy within UK higher education. However limited, this challenges socially committed scholars to consider whether they can use this narrow opening effectively to tackle social justice issues within their communities. In this chapter I argue that, despite the hurdles they face, black women academics have a unique opportunity to change the scope, discourse and agenda of research on black communities in the academy in ways that will lead to transformative outcomes.

The chapter unfolds in four parts: First, I interrogate the proposition that the modern university is a space for social change, since its foundations are built on racism and imperialism. In this context I address the dilemmas black academics face and suggest how they can take a transformative role. Second, I reflect on my personal journey within the UK academy as a scholar of Africa subjected to the continued coloniality of African Studies in the UK academy. Drawing on the experience of African Studies in North America, I reveal how changes can be made to the unequal power relationships between white and black scholars of Africa within the UK. Third, I explore the scope for Womanist learning within the academy, using my research on Africa to support an argument for an activist research agenda that challenges the coloniality of knowledge within the university. Finally, I discuss how black women academics might engage with black communities through scholarship and activism.

The modern university is not ours

As a space for knowledge production, the modern university has been a primary site in the struggle for black liberation, despite shrouding its discriminatory practices in modernist concepts of scientific objectivity, rationality and the universality of Western philosophy for understanding human societies. Furthermore, it is difficult to separate the establishment of the disciplines in the modern university from its association with the expansion of European empires and the consolidation of bourgeois hegemony under industrial capitalism. These social and economic changes required the dispossession and exploitation of those considered to be lesser humans, for which universities provided scientific justification, through views of eugenics, social Darwinism, moral climatology and development theories.

The modern university is undoubtedly a state project – one of the sites for the reproduction of capitalist, imperialist and patriarchal forces, and for the perpetuation of the global racial hierarchy associated with the Eurocentric culture of domination. It is with this knowledge in mind that African-American historian Robin Kelley (2016), debating the 2016 student activism in the USA, challenges those among the student activists who believe the university could be an enlightened space if it weren't for structural racism and patriarchy. Kelley argues that the fully racialized social and epistemological architecture upon which the modern university is built cannot be radically transformed by 'simply adding darker faces, safer spaces, better training, and a curriculum that acknowledges historical and contemporary oppressions'. 'Universities will never be engines of social transformation', he maintains. He urges us to look elsewhere, outside the modern university, for emancipatory spaces of activism, directing us to the 'undercommons', as articulated by Stefano Harney and Fred Moten (2013). As Kelley explains, 'the undercommons is a fugitive network where a commitment to abolition and collectivity prevails over a university culture bent on creating socially isolated individuals whose academic scepticism and claims of objectivity leave the world-as-it-is intact.'

More recently, in a UK media interview, black academic Kehinde Andrews (2016) states that the university is 'no less institutionally racist than the police', and comments that the problem faced by black people in the academy is far greater than can be solved by increasing the numbers of black and minority students and faculty, as universities do not produce knowledge that challenges racism (Ross, 2016). In effect, modern universities reflect and reproduce the power structures within society, providing the knowledge that state elites need to maintain their domination of economic, political and cultural life. Obviously, wherever universities are modelled on Eurocentric institutions (for example, in former colonial countries as in Africa and the Caribbean), their role is not to emancipate the people from imperial domination, nor to enable local elites to stay in power; instead, they act as conduits for international, often former colonial elites, to undermine and perpetuate the presumed superiority of Western science and the inferiority of local knowledge systems.

Student movements, such as 'Why Is My Curriculum White?' and 'Rhodes Must Fall', have questioned the very foundations of the knowledge that students are exposed to and are expected to acquire and reproduce within the academy (Chantiluke *et al.*, 2018). The hostile media and white academic reactions to such articulation for inclusivity and decolonial thinking from a small group of students disturbed and exposed the fragility of what appeared to be the secure ontological and epistemological basis of Eurocentrism in the academy.

These student movements have occurred at a critical juncture, in that the Anglo-American neoliberal phase of capitalism has undermined social democracy, enriched the wealthiest 1 per cent, and generated insecurities in all areas of life for the majority of people. The political and economic theories, whether classical or neoliberal, that have supported Western economic hegemony have been exposed as incapable of socially reproducing imperial societies without the extreme exploitation of dominated peoples abroad and at home. With no new direction, except a retreat to fascism, the political significance of the students' demands was manifested in the ferocity of the attacks on them by conservative scholars and the right-wing and liberal media.

The narrow and restricted openings in the Western academy for alternative epistemologies, be they indigenous, decolonial or Womanist can be partly attributed to the search for new knowledges in the commodification of knowledge. At the same time, attempts are being made to control the speed and direction of engagement with these new epistemologies through their co-option by normative [white] scholars. Sisters of Resistance (2018), two black UK academics, challenge the commodification of black struggles by white academics by asking: 'Is decolonizing the new black?' By that they mean: 'is decolonizing becoming familiar to power structures in ways that its consumption, circulation and reproduction in the academy is diluting its radical politics?'

My argument is that black academics, while battling micro-aggressions, should use their presence in the university to take from it what it offers. Here, I point to three things. First, the university enables us to confront directly the relationship between power and knowledge by giving us access to centres of imperial knowledge production and insights into how universities operate as spaces for the reproduction of Western modernity, which include the reproduction of racialized hierarchies and the exploitative practices linked to economic domination. We can envisage our academic labour as resistance – whether it is through diversifying the curriculum, supporting student movements or embracing research projects directly aimed at tackling social injustice. We can, as the pan-Africanist scholar Walter Rodney (1990) states, 'conduct an analysis designed to unsettle the relationship between white scholars and their younger white protégés', while also enabling our communities to learn transformative theories and practices in the struggles over ideas and for emancipation.

Second: the pedagogic role that we take on as tutors is particularly important in nurturing future scholars. We can, in the spaces where we work, introduce our students to alternative reading and non-Western knowledge systems, and diverse ways of knowing. We can encourage them to pursue knowledge beyond the established canon, in collaborative and community-based learning forums that draw on intersectional and emancipatory research ethics (Smith *et al.*, 2018).

Third, the university provides a space for critical analysis of areas in which marginalized people can develop the techniques of learning and knowledge production that could transform their lives. Here, Rodney (1990) urges us to remain in the academy, advocating that we should not enter institutions merely to gain legitimacy, but should become 'guerrilla intellectuals' (1990: 113) to 'operate in the aegis of the institution to take from it and transform it over time'. He recommends a work ethic that 'does not take the system too seriously' and asserts that 'we are working seriously to establish an alternative, as distinct from working seriously to participate in the system' (1990: 111). 'Guerrilla intellectuals' can work with communities, as their aim is to break down the distinction between intellectual and manual labour.

Being in the academy where your histories, societies and cultures are deemed unworthy of theoretical reflection and, when taught, not from the perspective of your people, can be disorienting – generating insecurities as to where you are coming from and what your future potential might be. This experience chimes with W.E.B. Du Bois's (1903) concept of 'double-consciousness'. Du Bois explains 'double consciousness' as 'a sense of always looking at one's self through the eyes of others, of measuring one's soul by the tape of a world that looks on in amused contempt and pity' (2008: 8). In effect, as Kwadwo Osei-Nyame Jnr (2009: 423) elaborates, you 'find that the initiative in your own life or your history is taken away. You are taken out of the stream of your own history and put into somebody else's'. We know the existence of alternative, non-Western ontologies that are important for realizing our potentialities, but our training in the modern university devalues them. According to Rodney, we need to 'find a way of mastering [bourgeois] knowledge from a different perspective' (1990: 114).

Doing African Studies as a black woman in the UK academy

As a British woman of African-Caribbean heritage and a pan-African feminist scholar studying African political geography, researching Africa presents numerous challenges relating to my race and gender that are exacerbated by the discriminatory practices arising from the coloniality of knowledge production on Africa in the academy in the global North. In the UK, African Studies is still dominated by remnants of the colonial elite and their protégés, who use white supremacy to access leverage to journals, funding and academic posts, while oblivious to the demands by black students and black academics for a change to the narrative on Africa, the epistemologies through which Africa is studied, and for greater access to the spaces in the academy (Daley and Kamata in Powell *et al.*, 2017). For example, journals with an Africa focus are predominantly based in the global North and studies have shown that articles by Africans in such journals are dismally low or even declining (Briggs and Weathers, 2016; Medie and Kang, 2018). Only a minute number of black academics in the UK work on Africa and even fewer sit on the editorial boards of major journals. This unequal geopolitics of knowledge production has been questioned since the 1960s.

It was only after intense struggles in the USA that black scholars were able to break the dominance of white Americans in the production of knowledge about Africa. This action was facilitated by the corpus of scholarship on Africa in the historical black colleges and the civil rights movement of the 1960s. Deep divisions emerged in the North America academy when the African and African-American scholars' greater presence challenged white domination of African Studies. Faculty became divided between Africanists (non-Africans who study Africa) and Africans/diaspora Africans. Michael West and William Martin (1999) write of the rival Africas and rival paradigms of Africanists and Africans at home and abroad. They note that white Africanists have 'long sought to separate sub-Saharan Africa, the object of their study and research agenda, from the African diaspora and the issues of race' (1999: 8). A similar argument can be made about white academics in the UK who view diaspora academics as not local to Africa and therefore offering nothing in terms of collaboration or insights into African societies. Many black academics were schooled within global North universities, so are also dismissed as being out of touch with the continent.

White academics in the UK have maintained their privileged positions in African Studies and in influencing government policy-making on Africa. Somehow, they have managed to ignore issues of race in the study of Africa, while reading the study of the continent through a racialized lens by denying the legitimacy of knowledge produced by Africans in the diaspora. My white students are often recruited as experts on topics that I have supervised them on. What I myself produce is seen as less legitimate, as it is perceived to be tainted with diasporic romanticism rather than with the claimed scientific objectivity of Western thought. Is our presence in the university, as Walter Rodney claimed, to validate the knowledge produced by others about us and to help that knowledge to evolve and, through so doing, garner professional validation?

African students coming to UK institutions are confronted with a disjuncture between their realities and the indignity of being taught about their continent by naïve tutors who claim superior knowledge of African societies. This attitude is more prevalent among white academics conducting research in former white settler colonies in Eastern and Southern Africa, where racialized hierarchies remain a persistent feature of everyday life, as Chapter 9 graphically illustrates. Further, discussion of their positionality is often avoided in their methodological statements. Yet we know that in the still racialized societies in Africa whiteness, and its association with global North donors, carries privileges that elude black academics, even locals (Pierre, 2013; Schroeder, 2012; van Zyl-Hermann and Boersema, 2017).

Decoloniality challenges the continued coloniality of the epistemic basis of knowledge about the global South and the reproduction of oppressive structures in a hierarchical order that is racialized, gendered, patriarchal and heteronormative, and that operates on multiple scales – from individual universities to the national, regional and global. Decolonizing African Studies is not just about incorporating African authors and worldviews, it is also about enabling the intellectual space for African and African diaspora scholars to be recognized as legitimate producers of knowledge about the continent.

As the decolonizing agenda has been taken up and seemingly commodified by white scholars in other disciplinary areas, Noxolo (2017a: 318) reminds us that 'decolonization begins from the scholarship of black and indigenous peoples and should be led by that scholarship'. In a discussion of the £1.5 billion that the UK government has taken off the aid budget to fund academic research linked to the United Nation's Sustainable Development Goals, Noxolo (2017b), notes that in the academic scramble for local collaborators 'decolonial theory can become yet another instrument for time-honoured colonialist manoeuvres of discursively absenting, brutally exploiting and then completely forgetting Indigenous people'.

Black scholars in the academy have to be attentive to ways in which black bodies are co-opted, commodified and strategically deployed by white academics. Black diaspora academics, especially women, have long realized the nuances of their struggles for emancipation. Since the nineteenth century (see African-American Sojourner Truth's 1851 speech 'Aint I A Woman') they have attempted to conceptualize their different experiences from white mainstream feminists, ones that reflect anti-racist and anti-sexist politics.

What then should be the role of a black Womanist in the academy? The concept of Womanism was coined by African-American author, Alice Walker (1983) in her book, *In Search of our Mothers' Gardens: Womanist Prose,* to signify 'a theory/movement for the survival of the black race; a theory that takes into consideration the experiences of black women, black culture, black myths, spiritual life, and orality – femininity and culture are equally important to the woman's existence' (1983: 27). Walker's intervention speaks to the thoughts of black feminists who have carved out their own space in feminism through academia and activism.

Space-making entails subversive action: disrupting scholarship and the binary between academia and activism. I propose that black women in UK academia are presented with three options: on the one hand, we can be complicit in the oppression of black people by doing slave labour; that is addressing the topics and the research questions that are in our oppressor's interests. For this we might be rewarded, but most often we become the black silent assistant/collaborator/partner – as the euphemism used to justify this unequal relationship becomes more sophisticated. In this labour we may side with other oppressed groups – such as feminists and non-binary people – but find ourselves fighting our battles on our own, as my experience of working with white feminist scholars reveals their unwillingness to bring race into the conversations when inequalities are discussed within the university. On the other hand, we may challenge the knowledge claims of our white colleagues. This does not happen without cost; we must be ready to accept unrewarding, marginal/insecure and precarious positions within the academy. Third, we may seek to do multiple labours – attending to the demands of Eurocentric knowledge gatekeepers, reaching the publications and teaching standards expected of our university, while at the same time trying to carve out a space in which we can generate alternative knowledges.

Our survival in the neo-liberal UK university requires the latter – undoubtedly a difficult position to occupy – as *we are in the university but not of it.* Josephine Beoku-Betts and Wairimū Njambi (2005) write that as African women in North-American universities they developed an awareness of how Africans are used to undermine African-American demands for representation, and they show how, through their teaching and by introducing black scholarship into the curriculum, they have challenged the students' and faculty's conception of their incompetence. It is a shame that within the academy exposing students to alternative literatures is still considered radical rather than foundational to critical inquiry. While black women have been 'guerrilla intellectuals', our space for critical activism has taken place outside the academy (Bryan *et al.*, 1985). Black women have largely written from spaces outside the academy in their struggles for liberation, as exemplified by the Combahee River Collective statement by black feminists in the USA in 1977, in which they state, 'we believe that the most profound and potentially most radical politics come directly out of our own identity, as opposed to working to end somebody else's oppression'.

For black women academics to engage with the African diaspora communities, they need to recognize the importance of belonging to a collectivity and nurturing the growth of that collectivity – a mechanism for progress recognized by African feminists (Steady, 2006). Beoku-Betts and Njambi (2005) note that one of the ways in which African feminism differs from Western feminism is the dichotomy between the individual and the collective. We know that as black women we cannot survive and carry out the tasks of reproducing life within the capitalist system without operating collectively, without drawing in the community – whether it is our sisters (biological and non-biological), families or churches etc. The importance of collectivity is counter to the neo-liberal university that fosters individualism, replacing the prima donnas of old with academic innovators/entrepreneurs in response to market-driven logics, and exhibiting accumulative practices not dissimilar to the corporate world.

Building and engaging with black communities

As Rodney argues, we need to know our local context before we can work to learn about others. Therefore, engaging with the community requires us to start with the one around us, in which we work and live. And in the space of the university the most immediate black community is that of the black students. Having suffered the alienating learning environments ourselves, we should use what little power we have to enable a more supportive space for black students. Some critics, including Kelley (2016), have argued that wanting safe spaces, religious spaces and psychological support may help individual students deal with everyday micro-aggressions, and are easy concessions for universities because they do not challenge the structure of the university itself. My view is that these safe spaces are critical to black students' well-being. However, they can only be successful if they are conducted as part of an attempt by the university to address how it is implicated historically and presently in racist ideologies and wider exploitative practices.

In effect, the resilience-building we seek has always come from within our networks and communities and always will. Therefore, working with black communities allows for reciprocity and mutuality. The community succours and strengthens us, and we in turn use the skills that we have developed to enable that community to tackle the social injustices that limit the fulfilment of our lives as human beings. First though, some of us need to begin by eliminating the distance between ourselves and the community. On a personal level, we have to challenge our own perception of our status *vis-a-vis* the community, and sometimes our own families' aspirations and perception of the ivory tower academic as inhabiting a space of aloofness, pride and privilege. Academics should be viewed as approachable and outward-looking, exhibiting mutuality and conviviality.

Through our determination to resist domination, we black women have devised methodologies that allow us to make linkages between what Patricia Hill Collins (2000) calls interlocking domains of power that together form a nexus of oppressive forces. Thinking in Womanist or intersectional ways allows us to produce knowledge that reflects and speaks to the lived experiences of our communities. I am advocating community building and collective responsibility at various places and across different scales. I suspect that my roots and families (as those of most black women in the academy, especially the first-generation immigrants) straddle various social classes, transnationally across the globe. It is our connections with these communities that make us important actors in emancipatory projects.

Our experiences are made up of multiple interconnected trajectories that operate across different spatial scales and times. I am interested in what such relationality does for political action. We have seen some solidarity movements scaling up to the global. I argue that African people in the diaspora have always been dependent on scale – imaginations of multiple scales – as a way of transcending and surviving exploitation, whether in dreams of the mother country, back to Africa, pan-Africanism or even to the Christian heaven. We have always looked for our emancipation beyond a bounded singular place. We are always reaching out to others who recognize our humanity and share our vision of the potentialities of just futures.

Hence, I see over 130 years of pan-African solidarity as exemplifying a black political/community movement that has been simultaneously local and global, connecting villages and towns in rural Africa to capital cities in networks of black internationalism. As academics we have the capacity to link people across these different scales and we need to reveal how, for example, a tube of skin-lightening cream does not just transform the person physically but is embedded in a mix of local and global racial and structural and corporate networks that serve to deny the beauty and thus the humanity of the user.

To exemplify from my own research: one of my interests is the embodied and relational politics of sexual violence in war and post-war societies in Africa and how hegemonic Western interpretations and policy frameworks actually serve to extend such violence by stereotyping men and women, objectifying the women and representing them as agentless victims who can only be empowered through the humanitarian action of Western women and former colonial states, involving Hollywood celebrity actors (Daley, 2015; Daley, 2017). These actions entrench spatio-racial and gendered hierarchies and disempower the women on whose behalf they claim to make interventions. Our work can articulate in the space of the academy what local people are already witnessing and thinking. Precisely that humanitarian missions are imbued with racialized, gendered and sexualized relationships that undermine whatever claim to moral and ethical responsibility they seek to uphold. Most Western scholarship on this issue continues to compound the oppression of African women.

In Daley, 2008, I demonstrate how intersecting oppressions of ethnicity, race and gender are sustained by militarism at different spatial scales (local, national, regional, global) to the extent that they can end in genocidal violence. My academic work seeks to transform scholarship on Africa and hopefully the realities of people's lives. The best accolade is when I get an email from someone in a country that I have worked on, who has read my work and is asking – how do you know or understand us so well? In response, I tend to draw on the philosophy of *Ubuntu* 'you are part of my community – your problems are mine – your well-being is mine. I am me because of you.'

Because my work situates racial hierarchies as preceding ethnic ones in the colonial state, many Euro-American scholars ignore it when they discuss Burundi. In my interpretation, this draws attention to their culpability. As Dionne Brand (2001) notes, the brave will say 'I was not there. I did not do this; why should I feel responsible for the past ... It never occurs to them that they live on the cumulative hurt of others. They start the clock of social justice only when they arrive' (p. 82). Righting academic and social wrongs in the global North requires that our academic work draws on a far longer historical trajectory, going back to the fifteenth-century 'voyages of discovery' when Europeans set out to capture resources for their country's enrichment, resulting in the genocide and enslavement of indigenous and black populations.

Hill Collins and Bilge (2016: 27–8) develop our understanding of relational thinking, in that it …

> rejects either/or binary thinking, for example, that opposes theory to practice, scholarship to activism or black to whites. The focus on relationship shifts from analysing what distinguishes entities, for example, the differences between race and gender, to examining their interconnections. Relationship takes various forms within intersectionality and is found in terms like *'coalition', 'dialogue', 'conversation', 'interaction'*.

Therefore, researching relationally involves the development of new methodologies that often require disrupting the discourse of the academy and opening ourselves up to unlearning and retooling.

From Black scholarship's engagement with the communities' new concepts, semantics and epistemes emerge to enable a better understanding and voicing of people's realities. The semiotics of the term *Womanist* is radical in framing and emancipatory in its teleology. Black scholars constantly construct new 'subversive' language to express the specificities of our condition, to signify our resistance and communicate our imaginations of a better future. By adopting concepts from the community, we can make much current academic language that does not reflect our worldview as redundant. In African Studies, that would mean dropping the colonial and donor language now in vogue, terms such as tribe, capacity building, self-reliance and entrepreneurship. Such language stifles creativity and the emergence of new and more radical ways of thinking about our conditions and potential. Donor frameworks address neither the struggles for human well-being nor the demands of people living under conditions of coloniality.

Another methodological way to work with the community is through the co-production of knowledge. This shifts knowledge production from its ivory tower pretensions and locates it within the places where people reside, thus overturning the hegemony of global North academics who add theory to data gathered from black bodies and lives, and recast them as objective knowledge. People-centred, grounded knowledge makes everyone an expert in something, empowering them to take transformative action. Through working collectively, black academics can create spaces for young black men and women to develop new tools of analysis that draw on our emancipatory histories and mobilizing practices in our centuries-long fight against white supremacy, patriarchy and economic marginalization.

Conclusion

Black people in the West have a 400-year history of activism against oppressive and exploitative economic and political structures that gained their legitimacy through the scholarship of the Western canon. Since the late nineteenth century, black people have articulated their resistance against empire through scholarly work that took place largely outside the academy. While some of this history has been documented, that of black British women's activism has received little attention. Documenting those resistance histories is important for black women in the academy who are seeking to link their research to community activism. By telling my history within the academy, I have shown how the field of African Studies continues to be implicated in the continuation of coloniality and white supremacy. I argue that student campaigns and the decolonial turn in the academy offer up opportunities for the few black women in the academy to disrupt and challenge hegemonic epistemologies and the geopolitics of knowledge production. Using Womanism as one possible theoretical framing, I have suggested conceptual and methodological ways in which black women's research can unsettle and transform how Africans in the diaspora do research on Africa, as well as engage with the issues faced within their communities in the UK.

References

Beoku-Betts, J. and Ngarũiya Njambi, W. (2005) 'African feminist scholars in women's studies: Negotiating spaces of dislocation and transformation in the study of women'. *Meridians*, 6 (1), 113–32.

Brand, D. (2001) *A Map to the Door of No Return: Notes to belonging*. Toronto: Vintage Canada.

Briggs, R.C. and Weathers, S. (2016) 'Gender and location in African politics scholarship: The other white man's burden?'. *African Affairs*, 115 (460), 466–89.

Bryan, B., Dadzie, S. and Scafe, S. (1985) *The Heart of the Race: Black women's lives in Britain*. London: Virago.

Chantiluke, R., Kwoba, B. and Nkopo, A. (eds) (2018) *Rhodes Must Fall: The struggle to decolonise the racist heart of empire*. London: Zed Books.

Combahee River Collective (1977) 'Combahee River Collective statement'. Online. https://tinyurl.com/y8bwz8lh (accessed 8 December 2019).

Daley, P. (2008) *Gender and Genocide in Burundi: The search for spaces of peace in the Great Lakes Region*. Oxford: James Currey.

Daley, P. (2015) 'Researching sexual violence in the eastern Democratic Republic of Congo: Methodologies, ethics, and the production of knowledge in an African warscape'. In Coles, A., Gray, L. and Momsen, J. (eds) *The Routledge Handbook of Gender and Development*. London: Routledge, 429–40.

Daley, P. (2017) 'Celebrities, geo-economics, and humanitarianism: The significance of racialized hierarchies'. In Frei, N., Stahl, D. and Weinke, A. (eds) *Human Rights and Humanitarian Intervention: Legitimizing the use of force since the 1970s*. Göttingen: Wallstein Verlag, 146–66.

Du Bois, W.E.B. (2008) *The Souls of Black Folk*. Oxford: Oxford University Press.

Harney, S. and Moten, F. (2013) *The Undercommons: Fugitive planning and black study*. Wivenhoe: Minor Compositions.

Hill Collins, P. (2000) *Black Feminist Thought: Knowledge, consciousness, and the politics of empowerment*. 2nd ed. New York: Routledge.

Hill Collins, P. and Bilge, S. (2016) *Intersectionality* (Key Concepts). Cambridge: Polity Press.

Kelley, R.D.G. (2016) 'Black study, black struggle'. *Boston Review*, 7 March. Online. https://tinyurl.com/jf8q6y2 (accessed 9 December 2019).

Medie, P.A. and Kang, A.J. (2018) 'Power, knowledge and the politics of gender in the Global South'. *European Journal of Politics and Gender*, 1 (1–2), 37–53.

Noxolo, P. (2017a) 'Introduction: Decolonising geographical knowledge in a colonised and re-colonising postcolonial world'. *Area*, 49 (3), 317–19.

Noxolo, P. (2017b) 'Decolonial theory in a time of the re-colonisation of UK research'. *Transactions of the Institute of British Geographers*, 42 (3), 342–4.

Osei-Nyame, K. (2009) 'Toward the decolonization of African postcolonial theory: The example of Kwame Appiah's In My Father's House vis-à-vis Ama Ata Aidoo's Our Sister Killjoy, Helon Habila's Waiting for an Angel, and Ike Oguine's A Squatter's Tale'. In Klein, T.R., Auga, U. and Prüschenk, V. (eds) *Texts, Tasks, and Theories: Versions and Subversions in African Literatures 3*. Leiden: Brill, 78–100.

Pierre, J. (2013) 'Race in Africa today: A commentary'. *Cultural Anthropology*, 28 (3), 547–51.

Powell, R.C., Klinke, I., Jazeel, T., Daley, P., Kamata, N., Heffernan, M., Swain, A., McConnell, F., Barry, A. and Phillips, R. (2017) 'Interventions in the political geographies of "area"'. *Political Geography*, 57, 94–104.

Rodney, W. (1990) *Walter Rodney Speaks: The making of an African intellectual*. Trenton, NJ: Africa World Press.

Ross, A. (2016) 'Universities do not challenge racism, says UK's first black studies professor'. *The Guardian*, 23 October. Online. https://tinyurl.com/zg5pdmo (accessed 29 November 2019).

Schroeder, R.A. (2012) *Africa after Apartheid: South Africa, race, and nation in Tanzania*. Bloomington: Indiana University Press.

Sisters of Resistance (2018) 'Is decolonizing the new black?'. Online. https://tinyurl.com/qpt8scm (accessed 8 December 2019).

Smith, L.T., Tuck, E. and Yang, K.W. (2018) *Indigenous and Decolonizing Studies in Education: Mapping the long view*. New York: Routledge.

Solanke, I. (2017) *Black Female Professors in the UK*. London: Runnymede Trust. Online. https://tinyurl.com/w9yn2h2 (accessed 8 December 2019).

Steady, F. (2006) *Women and Collective Action in Africa: Development, democratization, and empowerment*. New York: Palgrave Macmillan.

Van Zyl-Hermann, D. and Boersema, J. (2017) 'Introduction: The politics of whiteness in Africa'. *Africa*, 87 (4), 651–61.

Walker, A. (1983) *In Search of Our Mothers' Gardens: Womanist prose*. San Diego: Harcourt Brace Jovanovich.

West, M.O. and Martin, W.G. (1999) 'Introduction: The rival Africas and paradigms of Africanists and Africans at home and abroad'. In Martin, W.G. and West, M.O. (eds) *Out of One, Many Africas: Reconstructing the study and meaning of Africa*. Urbana: University of Illinois Press, 1–36.

Aspiration, exclusion and achievement: Reflections on black educational inequalities

Patricia Gilbert

Introduction

According to research by Demie and McLean, the educational attainment gap between British pupils of black Caribbean heritage and their peers is a persistent and ongoing problem with wide-ranging and complex causes. They argue that, despite the research evidence being available to address these inequalities, the 'school system has produced dismal academic results for a high percentage of Black Caribbean pupils' in England over the past six decades (Demie and McLean, 2017: 131). Within the higher education sector, concerns regarding attainment gaps have been given increasing prominence recently, particularly the gap between the percentage of black and minority ethnic (BME) students and white students obtaining an upper-second or first-class degree. These differentials particularly impact on black students, and gaps can be seen regardless of qualifications obtained prior to university. This chapter aims to provide an introductory discussion on black educational inequalities in the UK, with a particular focus on the history of concerns regarding the attainment of black Caribbean learners. It includes reflections on my experiences as a learner and educator, along with discussions about exclusion and under-achievement within schools and the BME attainment gap within universities. I conclude by considering calls to decolonize the curriculum and the potential that a more inclusive curriculum might have to transform educational institutions and mitigate against the inequalities of outcomes faced by black students today.

Context

I recently embarked on postgraduate studies as another step in my journey of lifelong learning, after teaching for several years in adult and further education, mainly as a sessional tutor, along with many other work roles. As a black woman of mixed heritage (black Caribbean and white British) from a working-class background, commencing a PhD focused on educational inequalities has led to a significant amount of self-reflection, not least on my position as a person 'embodying diversity' (Ahmed, 2009) often within a mainly white and middle-class academic environment. Discussing issues of race and racism can be challenging and can have a personal impact as you negotiate the discomfort and denials that the topic can raise. Ahmed describes the process by which the issue of racism can be diverted: 'In order to avoid people feeling bad, we have to make them feel good, by speaking about diversity. Our hurt and rage is blanketed under the warmth of diversity' (ibid.: 47).

Although I have witnessed a large amount of interest in, and commitment to, addressing educational inequalities from higher education colleagues, it has still been hugely important to me to be able to learn from other women of colour within academia and community activism, including those who have contributed to this publication, and to seek out black and other minoritized educators and activists committed to addressing racial inequalities. I have also found it impossible not to revisit my own experience as a black school pupil and higher education student as I carry out my research. I refer to some of these experiences below and to my personal journey as a learner, activist and educator, in the context of the past 50 years of black educational aspiration, exclusion and achievement.

School experiences

I attended primary school in West London in the 1970s, and while I remember not liking everything about school, I loved to learn and was often at the top of my class. Throughout my childhood, my Mum provided me with a constant supply of books, scouring sales and discount stores during the year to ensure a good stock for Christmas and birthday presents. We also spent plenty of time in the local library. By the end of primary school my parents were informed that I had one of the highest reading ages in my year, and I remember looking forward to getting regular homework when I started secondary school.

However, once at the senior school my enthusiasm for homework didn't last long; neither did my belief in my own abilities. Although unaware of the significance at the time, I had not taken up an offer of a place at a selective girls' school because I didn't want to go to a single-sex school after being bullied by other girls in junior school. In addition, my parents weren't keen for me to attend what was at that point an all-white school, no matter how honoured the headteacher told them they should be. My junior school head told them that I had only been chosen to help that school to diversify. So I went to the mixed secondary school that my older brother had also attended. The school had been formed by the merging of a secondary modern and a grammar school in the late 1960s. It was located in a very middle-class area but was socially and, to some extent, ethnically mixed. A hierarchy of classes existed, although they were never referred to as such by the teachers. My class was at the lower end of that hierarchy and consisted largely of children who, like myself, were from council estates in the surrounding areas. The teachers seemed to be obsessed with discipline, leaving little time to be enthusiastic about learning. Minor infractions, such as talking in line outside the classroom, could lead to quite disproportionate responses from teachers. I remember being dragged by my hair down the length of a corridor by a teacher for some such misdemeanour.

I remember only one teacher having any interest in my progress: an English teacher who stood out from the rest by engaging with the pupils as individuals. She was also the only person at school who I remember making a positive comment about my ethnicity, after years of experiencing the casual racism of the time. However, that feeling of being valued and encouraged was not repeated during the rest of my school career, which was dominated by my feeling unjustly picked on by teachers in the earlier years, and being ignored or barely tolerated as I moved up the school. Despite some good O-level grades, the school discouraged my parents from granting my wish to join the sixth form and take A-levels. It was suggested that a secretarial course would be more suitable.

Race, class and gender

As a schoolchild it was the intersection of race, social class and gender that impacted on my experience: to discuss one of these aspects of my identity in isolation from the others would give an incomplete picture. At no point in my school career was the prospect of working towards university entrance suggested as a possible route I could take. There was a pervasive expectation that I would take a traditional female and working-class role in clerical, retail or caring work. In her book, *Miseducation: Inequality, education and the working classes*, Diane Reay argues that despite the fact that the introduction of the comprehensive system was supposed to address class-based differentials, inequality has remained central to the system. This has been maintained by the retention of the segregation and elitism of the private school sector, the perpetuation of schools based on selection, schools whose catchment areas ensure working-class or middle-class majorities, and schools that utilize setting and streaming to mirror within them the former tripartite system, meaning that pupils within the same school can be offered very different experiences (Reay, 2017: 41). The largest 'gap' in attainment between different groups of school pupils remains that between those at the top and bottom of the socio-economic scale. Reay highlights Department for Education (DfE) statistics for 2013–14 that show that 36.5 per cent of students from disadvantaged backgrounds (which is defined as those eligible for the Pupil Premium) achieved five GCGE passes at grades A* to C, including English and Maths, compared to 64 per cent of students not considered to be 'disadvantaged', leaving a 27.5 percentage point gap (ibid.: 57).

However, since the ethnic monitoring of educational outcomes began, research has shown that differences in achievement between ethnic groups cannot be explained solely by disadvantage or social class, and investigations have identified a range of ways in which black pupils and students have been under-served by the British education system (Alexander *et al.*, 2015; Gillborn *et al.*, 2017). Arbouin's study, *Black British Graduates: Untold Stories,* analyses the educational experiences and career outcomes of a group of black graduates, who attended school in the UK in the 1970s and 80s. Despite their later success in higher education and professional careers, all of the participants in the study felt that they had not achieved their full potential in school and the majority did not achieve the government benchmark of school success (i.e. five GCSEs at grades A* to C, including English and Maths). Arbouin highlights the complexity of the relationship between social class, gender and ethnicity for black children, noting, for example, the lower average achievement of black boys from middle-class backgrounds compared to their white peers. Arbouin states:

> The most fundamental issue that emerged in discussion was the impact of poor teacher-student relationships, which were fraught with difficulties and underpinned by negative racial stereotyping. Boys felt that conflict with teachers affected their education. They were given significant encouragement for sports, but little for academic work … The girls were most affected by low teacher expectations and they found themselves streamed into lower-ability groups and given poor careers advice. (Arbouin, 2018: 114)

Like many of Arbouin's research participants, my journey to higher education included post-school study. Although I did enter sixth form, my experience there was characterized by feeling increasingly discouraged, aimless and out of place, and my poor attendance led to disappointing results. However, while my white, middle-class peers re-enrolled to improve their similarly unsatisfactory grades in order to apply for university places, the head of my sixth form made it clear to me that not only would I not be allowed to re-sit my failed exam, I would also, in her view, never go to university. Her words stayed with me for a long time, but a few years of uninspiring clerical work and an evening course later, I achieved my aim of commencing higher education. Despite increasingly high levels of black achievement, themes of low expectations, stereotyping and conflict are continuously uncovered in research on black experiences of education in the UK (Maylor *et al.*, 2009; Rhamie, 2012; Demie and McLean, 2017). These themes are also present in one of the foundational studies of discrimination towards black school pupils in the UK: Bernard Coard's study of the exclusion of black children from mainstream schooling in the late 1960s.

The scandal of the black child in schools in Britain

In 1971, Bernard Coard published *How the West Indian Child Is Made Educationally Sub-Normal [ESN] in the British School System: the scandal of the black child in schools in Britain*, exposing the deliberate over-representation of West Indian children in ESN schools. His analysis of the Inner London Education Authority's reports showed that twice as many 'immigrant' children were placed in ESN schools than the rest of the population, and three-quarters of these were of Caribbean background. Coard, a teacher in London ESN schools, undertook research that showed that in 19 such schools, headteachers estimated that between 10 per cent and 79 per cent of these children had been wrongly placed. Many parents had been led to believe that their children were placed in these 'special' schools in order to receive short-term extra help, but the reality was that only 7 per cent of the children returned to mainstream schools; the rest remained in schools where only a very basic education was made available. Children were placed in these schools on the basis of IQ tests, but Coard notes that the education authority recommended that many Caribbean children be placed in ESN schools even if they had a 'relatively high IQ'. Coard argued that the scores students obtained in the tests were lower than they should be, partly due to the cultural and middle-class biases implicit in the tests, and partly to the prejudice and patronizing attitudes of some teachers towards black children. Coard describes the 'entire racist context' and asserts that children can develop low expectations and low motivation, mirroring the low expectations that teachers had for them:

> The Black child acquires two fundamental attitudes or beliefs
> as a result of his experiencing the British school system: a low

> self-image, and consequently low expectation in life. These are obtained through streaming, banding, bussing, ESN schools, racist news media, and a white, middle-class curriculum; by totally ignoring the Black child's language, history, culture, identity. Through the choice of teaching materials, the society emphasises who and what it thinks is important – and by implication, by omission, who and what it thinks is unimportant, infinitesimal, irrelevant. (Coard, 1971: 31)

Nearly 50 years on, it could be argued that much of the description above is still relevant today, as are many of Coard's recommendations, including: addressing teacher expectations of black children; the need for more black teachers and educational psychologists; the continued role of community activism and supplementary schools; and the importance of teaching of black history and culture in schools for the benefit of all children, black and white. Coard's publication came out only three years after Conservative politician Enoch Powell's infamous rivers of blood speech. It was also only two years after American professor Arthur Jenson advocated different schooling for black children and white children, arguing that it was because of black children's 'genetically determined lower intelligence'. But despite the discrediting of the overt and scientific racism of Powell and Jenson, the wide recognition of the contribution of black people to all aspects of British life, along with racial discrimination legislation, black pupils are still affected by the impact of racist bias in education and wider society, as we can see in the differentials in exclusion, progression and attainment, discussed below.

Black underachievement: 'A matter of urgency'?

In 1977 the Select Committee on Race Relations and Immigration recommended 'as a matter of urgency' a high-level inquiry into the poor performance of ethnic minority children, particularly those of West Indian origin, prompted by the campaigns of Caribbean parents who had been raising concerns about the education their children had been receiving since the 1950s. A government Committee of Inquiry was set up, chaired by Anthony Rampton. In 1981 an interim report was published, entitled *West Indian Children In Our Schools* (although, as the report noted, 95 per cent of the 'West Indian' children were born in the UK). The inquiry had gathered evidence from Local Education Authorities and other organizations and individuals, including parents and pupils, and had undertaken 100 days of school visits. A sample survey of school leavers in six Local Education

Authorities found that of the West Indian leavers, 9 per cent received higher grades in English CSE and O level, compared to 34 per cent of all leavers. Similar differences were found for those achieving higher grades in Maths (Rampton, 1981: 9).

The report discusses the possible causes of 'underachievement', taking into account: parents' descriptions of the racism in schools and wider society and the teachers' low expectations of black pupils. The report goes on to state that the number of 'racist' teachers in school would likely reflect society and therefore be a minority; however, it found that 'unintentional racism' was more prevalent. The Committee found 'fairly widespread' views that West Indian children 'caused difficulties' and were 'unlikely to achieve in academic terms' (ibid.: 13). The report further notes that the 'colour-blind' attitude to students that some teachers advocated 'is in effect to ignore important differences between them which may give rise to particular educational needs' (ibid.: 13).

Modood and May note that some of the issues of concern raised in the interim report, including the teachers' 'negative racial stereotyping of ethnic minority students – particularly, African–Caribbean boys', and their lack of relevant training, proved too controversial for the Conservative government, leading to the resignation of the committee chair, Anthony Rampton, and his replacement by Michael Swann (Modood and May, 2001: 307). However, the ensuing Swann Report also recognized that underachievement was largely due to the discrimination and prejudice black children faced both inside and outside schools. It suggested that two issues needed to be addressed: 'eradicating the discriminatory attitudes of the white majority on the one hand and, on the other, evolving an educational system which ensures that all pupils achieve their full potential' (Swann, 1985: 768). This included enabling all students to understand what it means to live in a multiracial and multi-cultural country; not leaving this challenge to individual LEAs or just to schools with large numbers of minority ethnic students. These recommendations in the Swann Report sound radical today, more than 30 years later. However, it has been suggested that 'the idea of multi-cultural education was largely ignored by central government and only patchily experimented with by some local authorities and schools' (Modood and May, 2001: 308).

One response to the problems faced by black Caribbean children in schools was the burgeoning of black supplementary schools, which were held in the community outside normal school hours, and often run by volunteers. The schools have been described as standing in contrast to the 'dominant discourses of the urban working class, both black and white, [which] paint pictures of apathetic masses, inactive and uninformed (Mirza and Reay, 2003: 526–7). Mirza and Reay suggest that education can be seen as a 'consuming passion among the African Caribbean black British community' and 'educational urgency within the black community can be mapped at every stage of the educational process' (ibid.: 521). An urgency to address educational inequalities can also be seen in the attendance by thousands of black parents, students, teachers and others at the series of London Schools and the Black Child conferences, initiated by Diane Abbott, which took place between 1999 and 2014. An important topic at these conferences, and an area of ongoing concern to parents, is the disproportionate exclusion of black children from schools.

The school exclusions crisis

Over recent years, pupils of black Caribbean heritage have been three or four times as likely to be excluded from school as white pupils, although the group with the highest proportion of exclusions are students from Gypsy, Roma and Traveller backgrounds. The Institute for Public Policy Research reports that both black Caribbean and mixed-ethnicity (black Caribbean and white) pupils are disproportionately represented in Pupil Referral Units (PRUs) at nearly four times (3.9) and two and a half times respectively (Gill *et al.*, 2017: 18). They also state that there are more than five times as many children moved yearly to schools for excluded children than those officially recorded as being permanently excluded (ibid.: 9). The report notes that 'persistent disruptive behaviour' is the most common reason for recorded exclusions. In addition, tens of thousands of children are also believed to be subject to 'off-rolling': a form of 'illegal exclusion' in which children are removed from school rolls (ibid.: 9). The impact of exclusion on young people's health, qualifications, employment and criminality is outlined, including the greater likelihood of long-term mental illness and fewer than 1 per cent of excluded young people achieving five good GCSE passes including English and Maths (ibid.: 22). The report also notes that the majority of UK prisoners have been at least temporarily excluded from school and those who have been excluded are more likely to re-offend. While the report highlights the complex needs of all children subject to school exclusion, it draws attention to how black pupils are impacted by the intersection between ethnicity and factors such as poverty, the negative effect of racial discrimination on mental health; racist stereotyping and unconscious bias among teachers.

One statistic in particular from a 2012 inquiry by the Office of the Children's Commissioner highlights the shocking extent of the disproportionate exclusion of black children from school:

> If you were a Black African-Caribbean boy with special needs and eligible for free school meals you were 168 times more likely to be permanently excluded from a state-funded school than a White girl without special needs from a middle class family. (Office of the Children's Commissioner, 2012: 9)

The Commissioner, Maggie Atkinson, notes that while 'most schools work far beyond the call of duty to hold on to troubled and vulnerable children, a minority exclude on what seems to the observer to be a whim' (ibid.: 9). The research found discriminatory practice in three schools that excluded boys because of rules on hair length or rules on types of haircuts 'much more likely to be worn by one ethnic group' (ibid.: 99). Howarth (2006) states that her research uncovered 'symbolic exclusion': the experience black pupils had of 'feeling different, stereotyped, marginalized and discriminated against' before exclusions took place (ibid.: 2). One 15-year-old girl who was permanently excluded from a London school describes how her friendship group was considered to be a 'gang', unlike friendship groups of white girls. She also describes the process of being both 'highly visible' and invisible:

> But, you know, in the classroom, it was like the teachers could not even see us. When I put up my hand they would just look straight through me ... As soon as there's some noise, yeah, then the teachers look at the black girls. (Howarth, 2006: 2)

While some writers have also focused on issues such as peer relationships and sub-cultures (Sewell, 1997), differential treatment by staff and institutions remains a key issue, and the sense of being treated unfairly due to their ethnicity has been widely expressed by excluded black pupils (Wright *et al.*, 2005). John has suggested that:

> Tinkering with the system, amendments to the procedures and peripheral provision ... will not change things for black pupils generally. Those who have been subject to negative prejudice, destructive stereotyping and low expectations in the past will continue to suffer unless there are fundamental changes in schooling, a refocusing on children's education rights, and unless there is a halt to the present trend by government to make

excluding pupils easier than keeping them in the mainstream.
(John, 2006: 238)

It remains to be seen whether the *Timpson Review of School Exclusions*
(2019), with its recommendations to make schools more accountable for
excluded pupils, will address black children's disproportionate exclusion
and placement in alternative provision.

Measuring school achievement

In the summer of 2018 it was reported that Brampton Manor School in
East Ham, London, achieved outstanding A level results, with over 100
students achieving A or A* grades and 93 per cent of the A level students
achieving grades B and above; a record 20 students achieved places at
Oxford and Cambridge universities, all of whom had black and minority
ethnic backgrounds (BBC, 2018). The school had invested in preparatory
programmes for students applying for Oxbridge universities and 90 per
cent of its successful students were heading for Russell Group universities.
At the start of 2019 it was reported that a record 41 Brampton Manor
students had received offers from Oxford and Cambridge – 40 more than
had received offers in 2014; 'almost all' were from black and minority
ethnic backgrounds', many of whom were first in their family to go to
university, and more than half were eligible for free school meals (Busby,
2019). Headteacher, Dr Dayo Olukoski stated that:

> There is a huge talent within the BAME community and this
> number of offers is just attestation to the fact ... With self-belief,
> with determination, with the added support of school and home
> and the community – there is no ceiling to what you can achieve.
> (Drewett, 2019)

Stories of educational achievement such as these seem a world away from
concerns regarding 'underachievement'. Ethnic minority educational
success has been recorded for the past 30 years. Students of Indian heritage
surpassed the average attainment of white students in the 1990s (Gillborn
and Mirza, 2000: 10). In 2013, a greater proportion of black African
students achieved five GCSEs at grades A* to C than white students, and
pupils of Pakistani and Bangladeshi heritage have matched or exceeded
the attainment of white British pupils (Strand, 2015: 8). However, despite
the high levels of achievement of black and minority ethnic pupils from all
ethnic groups, differential average levels of attainment for black Caribbean
pupils still remain.

Gillborn *et al.* analyse the attainment of pupils with black Caribbean heritage over a 25-year period (between 1988 and 2013) and conclude that changes in government benchmarks of achievement have served to widen gaps for black students. They also note that decisions on entering pupils into the different tiers of GCSE exams has tended 'to exacerbate social inequalities', including adversely affecting the achievement of girls and disproportionately placing black students into foundation tier exams (Gillborn *et al.*, 2017: 859). Gillborn *et al.* argue that the goalposts have in effect been moved, as the benchmark of success has moved from five GCSEs at grades A to C in 1988, to the gold standard of 2005 that included higher grades in English and Maths, then to the English Baccalaureate (EBacc) in 2011 requiring two science subjects, one humanities subject and one language. Each change served to widen the achievement gap after progress in narrowing it had been made. They show that the application of the original benchmark for the 2013 GCSE results would result in its achievement by 82.7 per cent of white British students and 80.4 per cent of black Caribbean students: leaving a gap of just 2.3 percentage points (ibid.: 860).

The 2016/17 Department for Education statistics measure GCSE achievement in terms of the proportion of pupils achieving grade 5 or above in English and Maths, a score measuring performance in eight GCSE subjects (Attainment 8) and the achievement of pupils entered for the English Baccalaureate. In each of these measures, while several minority ethnic groups exceed the average attainment of white British students, students of black Caribbean heritage, including mixed white British and black Caribbean, have a lower average achievement than white British pupils: 28.7 per cent (black Caribbean) and 31.1 per cent (mixed white British and black Caribbean) pupils achieve grade 5 in English and Maths compared with 42.1 per cent of white British students (DfE, 2018). Demie and McLean note that 'the notion of Black Caribbean pupils' underachievement in British schools is in danger of becoming accepted as an irrefutable fact' (2017: 2).

However, the picture is more complex, as black Caribbean students eligible for free school meals (FSM) have a higher level of achievement than the white British students who are eligible, with 19.6 per cent achieving higher grades in GCSE English and Maths in 2016/17, compared with 16.9 per cent of white British pupils eligible for FSM (DfE, 2018). Attainment 8 scores are also higher for black Caribbean students eligible for FSM than for white British students who are eligible, with black Caribbean boys achieving an average score of 31.6 compared to 29.2 for white British boys (ibid). In addition, black Caribbean girls not eligible for FSM achieve a marginally higher Attainment 8 score than white boys in the same category (45.4 compared to 45.2), although they are behind white British girls not eligible for FSM, who score 50.4 (ibid).

Gillborn and Mirza's mapping of educational inequality in 2000 illustrated that 'even for the groups with the most serious inequalities of attainment nationally, there are places where that trend is being bucked' (Gillborn and Mirza, 2000: 9). In their analysis of local education authority (LEA) submissions for the Ethnic Minority Achievement Grant (EMAG), they found that black students were more likely to obtain five higher grade GCSEs than white students in nine LEAs, although in 34 the reverse was true (ibid.: 9). These differences based on location suggest that institutional factors are key. Demie and McLean note the complexity of the attainment inequalities affecting black Caribbean pupils, citing the extensive research that has identified stereotyping, low teachers' expectations, exclusions and poor leadership by headteachers as key issues (Demie and McLean, 2017: 3). They also echo the findings of research in previous decades, problematizing a 'colour-blind' approach that ignores the specific needs of black Caribbean pupils and a national curriculum that continues to fail to recognize the multi-ethnic nature of society (ibid.: 3–4). Lander's research with teacher trainees suggests that they are not properly prepared to teach in ethnically diverse environments, despite Qualified Teacher Status (QTS) Standards. She concludes that 'student teachers do not have a conceptual framework related to race issues' (Lander, 2011: 363). Maylor calls for teacher trainers and trainees of all ethnicities to be equipped to understand the biased perceptions and stereotypes that can impact on the attainment of black pupils, stating that:

> Ultimately, if teacher educators are to produce teachers who care that Black students are enabled to contribute to learning in the classroom, and achieve attainment goals in their examinations and future careers, they will need to teach in ways that transform student teacher consciousness and equip them to become critical educators. (Maylor, 2015: 31)

While the debate regarding school attainment continues, increasing levels of concern regarding differential outcomes in higher education have come to the fore over recent years, including the gap between the attainment of minority ethnic and white students, which can be seen across the sector.

The black attainment gap in universities

The 'BME attainment gap' refers to a comparison of the proportion of upper second-class and first-class degrees (termed 'good degrees') gained by UK-domiciled black and minority ethnic students in comparison to white students. A minimum classification of a 2:1 is increasingly required for graduate-levels jobs, as well as for post-graduate courses, putting students with lower grades at a disadvantage. AdvanceUK report that in 2017/18, 79.6 per cent of white UK-domiciled undergraduates received a first or a 2:1, compared with 66 per cent of ethnic minority UK-domiciled qualifiers: an attainment gap of 13.6 percentage points (2018: 114). The widest gap is between white and black students: 55.5 per cent of black students (comprising black African, black Caribbean and black other) achieved a first or 2:1, resulting in an attainment gap of 24.1 percentage points (ibid.: 114). The percentage of students achieving good degrees from all minority ethnic groups is lower than that achieved by white students, despite the higher average attainment of some minority ethnic groups in school statistics: 22.5 per cent of Chinese heritage pupils achieve at least three A levels at grade A or above, along with 15.3 per cent of Indian pupils, compared to 10.9 per cent of white students (DfE, 2018). However, both groups obtain a lower average of good degrees compared with white students – 5.0 and 4.5 percentage points less respectively – though these gaps are smaller than for several other minority ethnic groups (Advance HE, 2018: 137). For example, the average attainment of good degrees for students of Bangladeshi and Pakistani heritage is 13.1 and 14.9 percentage points below that of white students (ibid.: 137).

The percentage of students gaining a first or 2:1 in the UK increased by 19 percentage points between 2003/4 and 2017/18 (from 60.6 per cent to 76.6 per cent). The numbers of BME students gaining these classifications has also increased over that time (from 45.9 per cent to 66 per cent), but the gap between white students and BME students has remained quite steady over this period, reducing by only 3.6 percentage points (ibid.: 140). Similarly, the proportion of black students achieving good degrees has increased from 35.5 per cent to 55.5 per cent over the period, increasing by 20.3 percentage points, but the attainment gap has only fallen by 3.8 percentage points (ibid.: 140).

The 'BME gap' or 'black/white' gap provides stark figures that have galvanized the sector to address these anomalies. While factors such as prior educational qualifications are strong predictors of attainment, a gap exists even after accounting for these differences. Broecke and Nicholls' large scale cohort analysis for the Department for Education and Skills analysed a range of variables that could impact on the attainment gap, including 'gender, prior attainment (tariff score and type of level 3 qualifications), disability, deprivation, subject of study, type of HEI, term-time accommodation, and age'. It concluded that these could not account for all of the differences in outcomes seen between ethnic minority groups and white students (Broecke and Nicholls, 2007: 19). However, these national figures hide huge contextual variations. These can be seen across UK nations, with England having the largest attainment gap by ethnic group of 14.1 and Scotland the lowest, at 8.9 (Advance HE, 2018: 136). Differences exist between universities and types of universities: a report utilizing Higher Education Statistics Agency (HESA) data to show the difference in attainment across 20 institutions, showed that the size of the gap between white and black student attainment of a 2:1 classification varied from between 15 per cent and 29 per cent; the gap between the percentage of those two groups obtaining a first-class degree ranged from 21 per cent to 36 per cent (Buckley-Irvine, 2017). Differences in the size of the BME attainment gap can be seen between students studying SET (science, engineering and technology) subjects and non-SET subjects, and subject differences range from a 4-percentage point gap in medicine and dentistry to a 20-point gap in education (Advance HE, 2018: 114).

These figures suggest that institutional, subject and teaching practice may be key issues underlying these differentials in outcomes. While a gap in attainment has been shown to exist after other factors such as age and prior qualifications have been taken into account, these factors can make a significant difference to the size of the gap. For example, the attainment gap between BME students and white students aged 21 and under is 7.3 percentage points, compared to 15.3 percentage points for those aged 22 to 25 (ibid.: 190). In addition, while the 'gap' is usually measured by combining the average attainment of both first-class and upper second-class degree classifications, large differences in the attainment of each can be seen. For example, 42.7 per cent of black Caribbean students achieve a 2:1 in SET subjects compared with 45.8 per cent of white students, resulting in a gap of only 3.1 percentage points. However, this increases to a 19.1 percentage point gap in the achievement of first-class degrees (ibid.: 142).

At the end of 2018, the Office for Students (OfS) announced that all universities needed to eliminate the gaps in access and student success within 20 years. These included gaps in entry rates between the most and least represented groups in highly selective universities, gaps in drop-out rates, gaps in degree outcomes between white and black students, and between disabled and non-disabled students (OfS, 2018). Universities are implanting a range of initiatives and interventions to address ethnicity attainment gaps (UUK and NUS, 2019). Kingston University is a leader in the field, having increased the percentage of BME students achieving a good degree from 45 per cent in 2012 to 70 per cent in 2017; its focus on institution-wide change, building inclusive curriculums, and utilizing data, including a value-added approach, has been key to its success (Kingston University, 2017). One student-led approach that has gained increasing prominence in the sector is the movement to 'decolonize the curriculum', which builds on post-colonial perspectives and work over many years by anti-racist and black and minority ethnic scholars to promote the inclusion of black history in the curriculum.

Transforming institutions: Decolonizing the curriculum

When my older brother was in junior school, he received a class prize: an illustrated book about ancient civilizations. I was fascinated by the pictures and longed to learn more about other people in the world, past and present. One of my most cherished early memories is sitting looking through the atlas with my Dad as a child, and this 'global perspective' has continued to inform my personal, academic and political interests. However, I realized early on – as the illustrated book showed – that only some parts of the world were deemed worthy of comment. While the book covered civilizations from the Aztecs and Incas to the Etruscans and Romans, African civilization was represented by Egypt but the only person in the illustrations who appeared to be black was a servant in an Egyptian household. By the time I reached higher education, I found this absence of black people and perspectives seemed to characterize everything I studied.

For my humanities degree I chose a programme of politics, literature, history and philosophy. In many ways the degree course was exactly what I'd hoped for: every topic was a new and exciting challenge and I was to some extent able to satisfy my thirst for knowledge. However, ethnocentrism ran through all of the subjects I studied: this ranged from only white authors on modules in American and modern literature, to the sociology of the Third World, in which countless millions of people of colour were portrayed as passive victims of poverty and backwardness, to a history of eighteenth-century England in which, as my lecturer informed me, the study of the British slave trade was not relevant to the curriculum. However, within the exclusively white and male teaching staff that I encountered there were notable exceptions to this Eurocentric approach, including a lecturer who spoke about his lived experience of political struggle – from anti-Vietnam war protests to the miners' strike – and who taught a course on racism and politics. But I often felt, and acted, in opposition to the received wisdom being delivered, and felt compelled to seek out an alternative curriculum for myself; for example, learning about the history of black people in Britain and the British Empire through the works of Peter Fryer, or learning about black feminism through the works of Angela Davis.

Recently I've listened to black students from various institutions relating similar experiences to mine, decades after my undergraduate experience. For example, one student reported studying Joseph Conrad's *Heart of Darkness*, as I did at school in the 1980s, still with no opportunity provided for critical reflection on its deeply disturbing portrayal of African people or any meaningful presentation of writings on the topic of colonialism by African writers. In my teaching in adult education and access to higher education I have often been able to choose the writers to focus on and devise or amend reading lists, usually leading to classes that celebrated diversity and inclusivity, and received positive feedback from participants of all backgrounds. However, in UK universities in the twenty-first century, 'a simple request from a large number of students that their reading lists be broadened slightly to include some black and minority ethnic writers, becomes the basis of a manufactured racial "row"' (Gopal, 2017). A major broadsheet newspaper erroneously reported that Cambridge University was being 'forced' to remove white authors from the curriculum and replace them with black authors (Turner, 2017). The newspaper later retracted the claim, however, the student union officer, a young black woman whom they had identified as being responsible for 'removing' white authors (and pictured in their front-page article), went on to receive 'floods' of online racist and sexist abuse (Khomami and Watt, 2017).

hooks, reflecting on the critical and dismissive attitudes of some faculty staff to her Tony Morrison module, noted that they 'reveal how deep-seated is the fear that any de-centring of Western civilization, of the white male canon, is really an act of cultural genocide' (1994: 32). This fear can be seen in the hostile press reaction to student campaigns to decolonize universities and to any overt criticism of the role of the British Empire, such as the media storm in the press regarding the BBC's programmes commemorating 70 years of Indian independence in 2017 (Nair, 2017). In her 2017 blog article, 'Decolonizing the curriculum: what's all the fuss about?', Sabaratnam identifies three opportunities that the call to decolonize the curriculum provides: to look at 'our shared assumptions about how the world is', recognizing that many academic subjects were formed at a time when beliefs about racial inequalities justified colonial rule, which may have consequences for how the subject is taught; to consider the 'relationship between position and perspective' and how to diversify the sources used in scholarship; and to investigate 'the implications of a more diverse student body in terms of pedagogy and achievement' to ensure equality of opportunity for all students. In 2019, the National Union of Students and Universities UK released the findings of a sector-wide consultation with higher education students and staff. The report cites key factors relating to the attainment of Black, Asian and Minority Ethnic (BAME) students, such as: institutional culture, including the prominence of student deficit understandings of the issue; the lack of BAME staff, including role models and mentors; and a curriculum that fails to engage with 'issues of diversity, equality and discrimination' (UUK and NUS 2019: 17–18). The movement to 'decolonize' offers great potential for fundamental change in higher education, which could accompany other measures to tackle attainment gaps. However, the slow progress and retrograde steps in diversifying the school curriculum may have lessons that need to be considered.

Conclusion

When I reflect on aspects of black educational inequalities over five decades, I find it remarkable that so many themes are repeated in the research, which identify structural and institutional factors, yet individualistic and deficit understandings of these inequalities are still very prevalent. Despite the widespread acceptance of the findings of the Macpherson report, there appears to be little 'recognition that, like other institutions, universities are not immune from institutional racism' (Singh, 2011: 73). There is also little concerted effort to 'provide education which deals with racism awareness and valuing cultural diversity in the multicultural and multi-ethnic society in which we live' (Macpherson, 1999: 55). However, I also recognize the importance of celebrating achievement and change: from the increasing numbers of black and minority ethnic students entering and succeeding in higher education, to the role of community and family support in underpinning student success (Yosso, 2005; Rhamie, 2012), and the 'resilience' to disadvantage shown by black Caribbean and other minority ethnic students (Stokes *et al.*, 2015).

As the first person in my family to stay on at school past the age of 16, the issue of education inequalities based on social class is also important to me, even though attention to class is placed in opposition to attention to race in some discourses. One way to resist the attempts of those that seek to place white working-class educational underachievement in opposition to black and minority ethnic achievement, as if the latter causes the former, is, I believe, to focus on the need for 'high quality education for ALL' as Coard states in an article written 30 years after his ground-breaking pamphlet discussed above. Transforming the education system, Coard argues, is the foundation to addressing the 'poverty, racism, gender and class discrimination' and the 'income, wealth, social status and decision-making gaps which go with these in British society' (Coard, 2005: 184). The attempt to separate the interests of black and white working-class people is problematic, particularly when working-class students, black and white, can be affected by low attainment, low teacher expectations, and a lack of inclusiveness and role models (Demie and Lewis, 2014). However, it is hugely important that the specific educational inequities faced by black students are not subsumed by the wider issue of class-based inequalities.

While a Womanist approach can be interpreted in various ways, I am drawn to its 'liberatory' possibilities (Hill Collins, 1996) and focus on the intersections of class, 'race' and gender. Etienne (2016) encourages us to 'find our own voices' as black British women activists and academics, share commonalities of experience and ensure that our perspectives are not seen as marginal, but ones that can draw from lived experiences of racialized, classed and gendered positions in society, where active opposition to inequality and concern for community empowerment are often central. My journey through education, like that of many of the students I have taught, has not been 'traditional'. But now, having obtained higher education qualifications and having had the opportunity to help other people achieve their goals of entering and transitioning through higher education, sometimes after negative experiences of schooling, I look forward to undertaking further research in order to understand and contribute to countering these ongoing educational inequalities.

References

Advance HE (2018) *Equality + Higher Education: Students statistical report 2018*. London: Advance HE.

Ahmed, S. (2009) 'Embodying diversity: Problems and paradoxes for black feminists'. *Race Ethnicity and Education*, 12 (1), 41–52.

Alexander, C., Weekes-Bernard, D. and Arday, J. (eds) (2015) *The Runnymede School Report: Race, education and inequality in contemporary Britain*. London: Runnymede Trust.

Arbouin, A. (2018) *Black British Graduates: Untold stories*. London: Trentham Books.

BBC (2018) 'Brampton Manor school's record A-level results'. *BBC News*, 16 August. Online. www.bbc.co.uk/news/uk-england-london-45209847 (accessed 29 July 2019).

Broecke, S. and Nicholls, T. (2007) *Ethnicity and Degree Attainment* (Research Report RW92). London: Department for Education and Skills.

Buckley-Irvine, N. (2017) 'Universities' shame – unpicking the black attainment gap'. *Wonkhe*, 10 August. Online. https://tinyurl.com/t9h2ce3 (accessed 9 December 2019).

Busby, E. (2019) 'State school in one of London's poorest boroughs secures 41 offers to study at Oxford and Cambridge universities'. *The Independent*, 17 January. Online. https://tinyurl.com/ydcmy566 (accessed 29 November 2019).

Coard, B. (1971) *How the West Indian Child is Made Educationally Sub-Normal in the British School System*. London: New Beacon Books.

Coard, B. (2005) 'Thirty years on: Where do we go from here?'. In Richardson, B. (ed.) *Tell It Like It Is: How our schools fail black children*. London: Bookmarks Publications, 184–91.

Demie, F. and Lewis, K. (2014) *Raising the Achievement of White Working Class Pupils: Barriers and school strategies*. London: Lambeth Research and Statistics Unit.

Demie, F. and McLean, C. (2017) *The Achievement of Black Caribbean Pupils: Good practice*. London: Lambeth Education and Learning.

DfE (Department for Education) (2018) *Revised GCSE and Equivalent Results in England, 2016 to 2017* (SFR01/2018). London: Department for Education.

Drewett, Z. (2019) 'State school where 41 students are going to Oxford and Cambridge'. *Metro*, 17 January. Online. https://tinyurl.com/trem9d4 (accessed 29 November 2019).

Etienne, J. (2016) *Learning in Womanist Ways: Narratives of first-generation African Caribbean women*. London: Trentham Books.

Gill, K., Quilter-Pinner, H. and Swift, D. (2017) *Making the Difference: Breaking the link between school exclusion and social exclusion*. London: Institute for Public Policy Research.

Gillborn, D., Demack, S., Rollock, N. and Warmington, P. (2017) 'Moving the goalposts: Education policy and 25 years of the black/white achievement gap'. *British Educational Research Journal*, 43 (5), 848–74.

Gillborn, D. and Mirza, H.S. (2000) *Educational Inequality: Mapping race, class and gender: A synthesis of research evidence*. London: Office for Standards in Education.

Gopal, P. (2017) 'Yes, we must decolonise: Our teaching has to go beyond elite white men'. *The Guardian*, 27 October. Online. https://tinyurl.com/yaurf6e9 (accessed 29 November 2019).

Hill Collins, P. (1996) 'What's in a name? Womanism, black feminism, and beyond'. *The Black Scholar*, 26 (1), 9–17.

hooks, b. (1994) *Teaching to Transgress: Education as the practice of freedom*. New York: Routledge.

Howarth, C. (2006) 'School exclusion: When pupils do not feel part of the school community'. *Journal of School Leadership*. Online. http://eprints.lse.ac.uk/id/eprint/15346 (accessed 29 July 2019).

John, G. (2006) *Taking a Stand: Gus John speaks on education, race, social action and civil unrest 1980–2005*. Manchester: Gus John Partnership.

Khomami, N. and Watt, H. (2017) 'Cambridge student accuses Telegraph of inciting hatred in books row'. *The Guardian*, 26 October. Online. https://tinyurl.com/y8y3uumh (accessed 29 November 2019).

Kingston University (2017) 'New figures cement Kingston University's role as sector champion in nationwide bid to close BME attainment gap'. Online. https://tinyurl.com/qmrz8tk (accessed 9 December 2019).

Lander, V. (2011) 'Race, culture and all that: An exploration of the perspectives of white secondary student teachers about race equality issues in their initial teacher education'. *Race Ethnicity and Education*, 14 (3), 351–64.

Macpherson, W. (1999) *The Stephen Lawrence Inquiry*. London: The Stationery Office.

Maylor, U. (2015) 'Challenging cultures in initial teacher education'. In Alexander, C., Weekes-Bernard, D. and Arday, J. (eds) *The Runnymede School Report: Race, education and inequality in contemporary Britain*. London: Runnymede Trust, 27–31.

Maylor, U., Smart, S., Kuyok, K.A. and Ross, A. (2009) *Black Children's Achievement Programme Evaluation* (Research Report DCSF-RR177). London: Department for Children, Schools and Families.

Mirza, H.S. and Reay, D. (2000) 'Spaces and places of black educational desire: Rethinking black supplementary schools as a new social movement'. *Sociology*, 34 (3), 521–44.

Modood, T. and May, S. (2001) 'Multi-culturalism and education in Britain: An internally contested debate'. *International Journal of Educational Research*, 35 (3), 305–17.

Nair, A. (2017) '"More c**p, more bias!": Viewers fume over "UK bashing" on BBC Newsnight Partition special'. *The Express*, 16 August. Online. https://tinyurl.com/tcnojpz (accessed 29 November 2019).

Office of the Children's Commissioner (2012) *"They Never Give up on You": Office of the Children's Commissioner School Exclusions Inquiry*. London: Office of the Children's Commissioner.

OfS (Office for Students) (2018) 'Office for Students: Universities must eliminate equality gaps'. Online. https://tinyurl.com/yx5wbwpc (accessed 9 December 2019).

Rampton, A. (1981) *West Indian Children in Our Schools*. London: HMSO.

Reay, D. (2017) *Miseducation: Inequality, education and the working classes*. Bristol: Policy Press.

Rhamie, J. (2012) 'Achievement and underachievement: The experiences of African Caribbeans'. *Race Ethnicity and Education*, 15 (5), 683–704.

Sabaratnam, M. (2017) 'Decolonising the curriculum: What's all the fuss about?'. SOAS blog, 18 January. Online. https://tinyurl.com/u9f6thc (accessed 9 December 2019).

Sewell, T. (1997) *Black Masculinities and Schooling: How black boys survive modern schooling*. Stoke-on-Trent: Trentham Books.

Singh, G. (2011) *A Synthesis of Research Evidence: Black and minority ethnic (BME) students' participation in higher education: Improving retention and success*. York: Higher Education Academy.

Stokes, L., Rolfe, H., Hudson-Sharp, N. and Stevens, S. (2015) *A Compendium of Evidence on Ethnic Minority Resilience to the Effects of Deprivation on Attainment: Research report*. London: Department for Education.

Strand, S. (2015) *Ethnicity, Deprivation and Educational Achievement at Age 16 in England: Trends over time: Annex to compendium of evidence on ethnic minority resilience to the effects of deprivation on attainment*. London: Department for Education.

Swann, J. (1985) *Education for All: The report of the Committee of Inquiry into the Education of Children from Ethnic Minority Groups*. London: HMSO.

Timpson, E. (2019) *Timpson Review of School Exclusion*. London: Department for Education.

Turner, C. (2017) 'Cambridge to "decolonise" English literature [corrected]'. *The Telegraph*, 24 October. Online. https://tinyurl.com/w4f6b3f (accessed 9 December 2019).

Universities UK and NUS (National Union of Students) (2019) *Black, Asian and Minority Ethnic Student Attainment at UK Universities: #ClosingtheGap*. London: Universities UK and National Union of Students.

Wright, C., Standen, P., John, G., German, G. and Patel, T. (2005) *School Exclusion and Transition into Adulthood in African-Caribbean Communities*. York: Joseph Rowntree Foundation.

Yosso, T.J. (2005) 'Whose culture has capital? A critical race theory discussion of community cultural wealth'. *Race Ethnicity and Education*, 8 (1), 69–91.

Chapter 4

Hello trouble! Black women academics and the struggle for change

Cecile Wright

Introduction

'Hello Trouble!' That's the way I'm greeted by some people who are white. The tone is usually light-hearted and superficial. However, the frequency of this greeting has led me to reflect upon the use of the word 'trouble' to suggest that I say things the speaker doesn't approve of. Or I do things the speaker doesn't approve of. Is the greeter suggesting that I should toe the line, not upset the applecart, accept the status quo and above all know my place (as David Lammy MP said in the House of Commons when referring to the Windrush scandal) (Hansard, 18 May 2018)? Patricia Williams (2018) expresses similar themes:

> Lack of civility is underwritten by broad habits of courtesy that dictate whose voices count; which bodies are or are not capable of speech, witnessing, forming opinion. Who speaks to whom? Who is spoken of? Who do we horrify into silence? And among the voices most insistently suppressed written off and written out are those of black women and girls. (Williams, 2018: 1)

I, along with many Black women academics, have experienced this positioning in my working life in the academy (Wright *et al.*, 2007, 2018).

This chapter engages with my work as an activist and academic to give a voice to the otherwise voiceless. Such work specifically focuses on Black youth in Britain and their struggles in education. It illustrates the Womanist mantra 'the personal is political' (Hill Collins, 1990) and recognizes the extent to which Black women academics are inextricably linked to their communities (hooks, 1989, 1992). It covers over three decades of research and scholarship in the field, which not only calls out, confronts and resists the negative hegemony of Britain's Black community but illuminates the Black community's ways of being that inspire healing and transformation.

Indeed, Katy Sian (2017: 2) asserts:

> Racism across British universities inevitably takes its toll on academics of colour who carry the heavy burden of precarity as they are more than often positioned as outsiders. This weight is made increasingly heavier against a backdrop of an unforgiving neoliberalization in which universities precipitously compete over performance, student satisfaction scores, Research Excellence Framework (REF) rankings, and student recruitment figures. These rapid changes place academics of colour at greater risk, who alongside keeping up with new needs and demands, must also continue to put up with embedded practices of racism. (Sian, 2017: 2)

Challenging and overcoming institutional oppression

Despite the rhetoric by the academy of its commitment to social justice, the experience of Black women reveals a clear pattern of institutional oppression (hooks, 1992). This occurs as a result of being in spaces that were not intended for them (Lorde, 1984).

Little appears to have changed. Wright *et al.* (2018: 70), in highlighting the profile of the British academy refer to the sheer weight of whiteness. Researchers have identified invisibility as a major issue for Black women academics in the UK. Wijeyesinghe and Jones (2013) contend that on predominantly white campuses, Black women academics 'may experience both invisibility as result of intersections of race and gender, as well as heightened visibility in contexts in which they clearly are the minority compositionally' (2013: 138). In Britain, Black female academics are often rendered invisible and their entry into the academy conditional because they are considered inauthentic. The near absence of Black women in senior positions encourages assumptions of limited competence and lack of entitlement to membership.

Notwithstanding these challenges, Black women in academia have for decades been at the forefront of women's struggle for social justice (Perlow *et al.*, 2018) through, for instance, generating knowledge about the Black community as a political endeavour aimed at creating research that offers a voice for the voiceless. However, because Black women are often engaged in academic work critical of the status quo, success goes unrecognized (hooks, 1992). Nevertheless, Black women in academia maintain their activism to effect change (Perlow *et al.*, 2018).

For instance, Black academic work in the humanities and social sciences has sought to demonstrate a clear break with dominant epistemological frameworks that pathologize the Black community and over-emphasize that which devalues it and reinforces Black women's status as devalued victims (hooks, 1989) instead of highlighting their significant change-making efforts:

> Even if perceived 'authorities' writing about a group to which they do not belong or over which they wield power, are progressive, caring and right-on in every way, as long as their authority is constituted either by the absence of the voices of the individuals whose experience they seek to address, or the dismissal of those voices as unimportant, the subject/object dichotomy is maintained and domination is reinforced. When we write about experiences of a group to which we do not belong, we should think about the ethics of our action, considering whether or not our work will be used to reinforce and perpetuate domination. (hooks, 1989: 43)

This raises questions about the notion of the objective researcher and demands a positioning of academia firmly within communities as part of their struggles rather than as distant observers or outside commentators.

The nature of the activism of black women academics

In the US the role of Black women as leaders of social movements has been less recognized than that of Black men (Williams, 2017). Yet historically, Black women within the US academy have produced more scholarly liberatory work to effect social change in tandem with activism (Perlow *et al.*, 2018) than Black women academics in the UK (hooks, 1995, 2003). There is a greater presence of Black women in US universities (Wright *et al.*, 2018) and various explanations for this can be postulated, including independent national civil rights movements in the US that Black female academics could be involved in (Davis, 1981, Walker, 1983, Hill Collins, 1990). These movements had substantial publicity and a pronounced effect. Moreover, the recent founding of Black Lives Matter by Black women in the US highlights not only the ways they contribute to leading powerfully effective protest, but also their long history as key players in movements for social justice (e.g. Williams, 2017; Toone *et al.*, 2017; Perlow *et al.*, 2018).

By contrast, much of Black women's activist work within Britain has taken the form of public political activity such as protests, and has existed outside the academy structures (see Bryan *et al.*, 1985; Mirza, 1997;

Etienne, 2016; Bassel and Emejulu, 2017). For instance, prominent Black women activists and campaigners in Britain have been catalysts for societal and institutional change that inspire both healing and transformation. Claudia Jones is one historical example. Shortly after arriving in England in 1955 she became actively involved with the Black community to campaign against racism in housing, education and employment. She later addressed peace rallies and helped organize campaigns against the 1962 Immigration Act. She recognized that black people needed a voice and founded and edited the first Caribbean journal in the UK, *West Indian Gazette*. She was an early contributor to the establishment of a Caribbean Carnival, precursor of, the Notting Hill Carnival. Doreen Lawrence, mother of Stephen Lawrence, the Black teenager murdered in a racist attack in south-east London in 1993, is another effective activist. She has been a powerful campaigner who has driven reforms to the police service and aspects of the criminal justice system.

The Womanist mantra: Resisting marginalization and fighting for community

At the heart of my work as a scholar-activist is an attempt to break with dominant epistemological frameworks, which within the academic literature constructs Blackness as being associated primarily with social problems. The catalysts for claiming my educational space and deploying a distinctively grassroots perspective in the knowledge production that emanated from my time as a student were my contact with two important multi-authored books: *The Empire Strikes Back* (1982) and *The Heart of the Race: Black women's lives in Britain* (1985). In *The Empire Strikes Back*, Errol Lawrence argued that white sociology in Britain was complicit in reproducing a Black pathology, and was unable to describe the rich and complex cultural experience before them. And in *The Heart of the Race*, the three Black women authors challenged the official narratives and constructions of race, gender and class; in particular, a racial discourse where the subject is male, a gender discourse in which the subject is white, and a class discourse that deemed race invisible. In addition, Black people were feared through perceived acts of public/social disorder but this often correlated Blackness with masculinity and therefore served not only to omit the Black female experience but to demonize Black men.

After I read these two books, my own work began to challenge accepted notions about the Black community. For instance, some of my empirical work about the educational experiences of Black children in British schools (Wright, 2005) challenged status quo assumptions around Black families and the abilities of Black children. In this sense my findings were troubling for the established views about the underachievement of Black children. Drawing upon black feminist frameworks and epistemologies to reframe the questions and assumptions about the Black community, my work exemplifies how academics and researchers can, as activists, contribute to those struggles, particularly as academia is increasingly under pressure to demonstrate the relevance and impact of its research but also its limitations and challenges.

Within British higher education, in defiance of Audre Lorde's (1984) observation that Black women were never meant to survive in the academy, they have endeavoured both to transform it (e.g. Wright, 2007, 2018) and produce counter narratives that challenge deficit thinking about the Black community and women's intellectual production.

Notwithstanding their struggle in predominantly white higher education institutions, alongside 'scholarly liberatory work to effect social change', Wright *et al.* (2018) describe how…

> bringing community networks from the margins into the centre of higher education challenges the invisibility of Black workers. Black women's intentional visibility extends beyond their mere presence in UK universities. It also includes advocating on behalf of their Black sisters, brothers, children, and the next generation of Black students, through their work and affiliations to professional networks. (Ladson-Billings, 2005; Wright *et al.*, 2007)

Transforming the educational experiences of black youth

A recent newspaper article (Motune, 2018) reported the latest statistics from The Universities and Colleges Admissions Service (UCAS). They show an increase in the number of young black people of African Caribbean background applying to university, particularly to the Russell Group. These statistics are significant. Firstly, they counter the discourse of black children's attainment over the last 60 years, which has consistently pathologized them in education and wider policy debates as disinterested in education. This is despite the analyses of school attainment data in English schools showing that from the start of primary school to the completion of secondary education, children from Black Caribbean backgrounds tend to fall back, rather than progress, over the course of their schooling (Wright, 2013). The statistics are emblematic of the struggle to transform the education system through education initiatives that have their genesis in Black communities.

My work in this area is based on qualitative research methods focused on the experience of young Black people at micro levels, highlighting their lives in classrooms and schools. I invoke a range of theories and epistemologies, including critical race theory, Black feminist thought, Womanist theory and postcolonial theory. In an attempt to reframe the persistent positioning of Black youth as a problem, I pose research questions relating to young Black people's schooling experiences. These questions include: What role does the intersection of race, gender and class play in the education of young Black people? What do we understand by the pattern of exclusion from education that results from their schooling experiences, and the subsequent cultural nuances? Most importantly, how do Black young people and their families transform their educational experiences?

Such questions posed by a Black woman in the academy can be perceived as troublesome, bold and out of place, because they are designed to transmit oppositional knowledge to counter white supremacist and patriarchal hegemony, and to create positive, deep structural shifts in worldviews, ways of being, and actions (Perlow *et al.*, 2018: 2).

The extracts from two articles below illuminate the narratives relating to the Black young people lives in classrooms and schools. The article concerning race and gender, contesting and resistance in schooling (Wright and Weekes, 2003: 3–20) is focused on data gathered as part of an ethnographic study of secondary school exclusions conducted in five secondary schools. The narratives of young Black women relate to the introduction of a new change in classroom discipline. Some of them felt that this had an adverse effect on them. Some felt that the headteacher spoke to them disrespectfully so they reacted negatively. And the cycle continued. The young women felt the headteacher's tightening up of discipline was racialized, and reacted by using racial signifiers such as kissing their teeth.

The young women felt that reporting racism achieved nothing and they resented this disregard. They also felt they were singled out for bad behaviour when others were the culprits. Though this was indicative of their powerlessness, they still verbally challenged decisions they felt to be wrong. The examples below illustrate how they felt.

'He calls everyone a clown and only excludes black people. He must think we'll react in a certain way to that. We're bound to react in a bad way.'

'When I can see racism staring in my face and I can see him treating the [white] people different and I just flip and just cuss him off.'

'We report it and no-one does anything. So they wonder why we turn bad.'

The young women felt racism was endemic within their school experience and that they needed to devise forms of resistance against these daily encounters. Yet they recognized the dichotomy posed by their response to the processes of racialization, which ultimately created ongoing conflict between themselves and the school.

A crucial element in the young women's narrative is their complaint about the scrutiny that accompanied their hyper-visibility, which made them disproportionately subjected to the school's disciplinary processes. Additionally, they understood how power operates across gender, race and class as an intersecting system of power, as well as how power organizes the institution's disciplinary practices, cultural practices and interpersonal relations throughout their schooling. Their narratives also revealed the strategies young Black women employed for survival and resistance, strategies that included the deployment of overt racial signifiers.

The second article (Wright, Maylor and Becker, 2016: 21–34) illuminates how black oral history traditions, critical race theory and Black feminist frameworks and epistemologies (e.g. Hill Collins, 2000) coalesce. Together they help to break the dominant epistemological framework that over-emphasizes young Black men's status as devalued victims, while revealing positive narratives of educational success.

The poor educational participation and lack of academic success of Black boys and men in compulsory schooling and higher education is both a current and longstanding issue in the Global North and South (NCES, 2018). In the UK a plethora of research and publications since the 1970s have focused on the underperformance of young Black males in the British education system. Black males of African Caribbean origin are among the lowest performing students in Britain: they achieve some of the lowest grades and have the highest likelihood of being excluded from school.

However, some young Black males are able to achieve against the odds, that is, to navigate successfully through compulsory education and then go on to higher education – a social marker for academic success and a prelude for social mobility. But how do they succeed and what contributes to their success? The objective of the study was to explore the positive factors, which yielded information and insight about these males' academic success. The study addresses how these young Black males deploy agency, resilience and the turnaround narrative in order to challenge their label as educational failures and achieve against the odds. It argues that perceptions of Black masculinity have been associated with academic underperformance, yet that they are able to recover from failure through agency, resilience and the turnaround narrative (Harding, 2010). The turnaround narrative describes a narrative embodied by recognizing previous errors that caused setbacks or failures and instead pursuing recovery and redemption. Despite finding themselves in a failing situation, such as permanent or temporary exclusion, these young Black males are not deterred from pursuing educational attainment; rather they show determination to succeed, which is, in turn, cultivated by their family and organizational or community agents. Essentially, despite low educational attainment, some young black males make new efforts to progress through education, thereby demonstrating their agency and resilience:

> I need to go back to college, go to school and don't get kicked out. It's not good in the long run ... it's hard to find a decent job without qualifications.

This narrative is suffused with notions of culture, individual agency, familial and community responsibility, subjectivity and becoming. His narrative suggests why, despite low attainment at age 16, young Black people participate disproportionally more in higher education than their white peers. Overlooking the differential outcomes of ethnic minorities in education, the drive for social progression through educational attainment is demonstrated by the fact that while ethnic minority communities account for 8 per cent of 18–24-year-olds in Britain, they make up almost twice this proportion of university entrants (Shiner and Modood, 2002: 210).

> They [my family] kept me up and encouraged me a lot ... they were always there for me and from the beginning they believed in me. (Shiner and Modood, 2002: 210)

This young man spoke of the pivotal role played by his family in transforming a negative educational experience and the endeavour to forge success:

> I just have a team that is trying to support the young people for what they have been through and supposed to get and have been denied, and try to do the best we can do within the parameters and move the boundaries and knock the door hard and move the doors off the hinges to make changes.

Reynolds (2008) suggests that localized community programmes such as those offered by Black community organizations, churches etc., play a pivotal role in ameliorating the effects of the social exclusion of young Black people. It should be recognized that despite the apparent problems associated with Black locality, such as poverty or limited social mobility, these spaces hold intrinsic value in the lives of young people.

In sum, my work in this area illustrates how the young people, parents and the community recognized that schools and teachers were gatekeepers to educational success. For instance, by invoking Black cultural capital, the young people subscribe to a complex class curriculum, which requires planning (with parents), practising (at home or Saturday/supplementary school). These components contribute to their success and act as a corrective to the dominant hegemony that pathologizes Black youth and their families.

Conclusion

This chapter began with a focus on the suppression and invalidation of Black female voices. This occurs in general societal forums with an implication that anything said should be dismissed or not taken seriously.

The specific forum addressed in this chapter is in the workplace of academia. Seats of learning are not only institutions where Black women are located in spaces not intended for them and are in effect invaders in these spaces. If these spaces were not intended for them, not devised or developed for them, their presence can be seen as alien or unacceptable to others. Despite this, Black women have struggled and resisted their othering in academia. This is evidenced in their work, which offers a voice to otherwise voiceless Black communities.

Black women in the US have combined academic work with activism, visibly more so than their peers in the UK academy. In the UK, Black women have been absent as national figures, 'leaders' or major players in the movements for social justice. In recent years a prominent Black woman who has gained frequent attention, Diane Abbott, Member of Parliament, has frequently been ridiculed in the media and thus undermined (Wright, 2017). Within the British academy Black women have produced intellectual work that challenges their non-acceptance and othering. They have combined challenging their invisibility as academics with advocating on behalf of other Black workers and students.

My own work has centred on giving a voice to young Black people. *Black Youth Matters* challenges the dominant discourse of Black children's disinterest in education. This is despite the evidence that their underachievement mainly begins in secondary school, not primary school. It is in secondary school (11–18) that Black children experience disproportionately high rates of exclusion and negative labelling. The narratives of young Black women are filled with the disrespect they encounter and how they feel singled out for behaving badly. Their hypervisibility and belittlement in school are echoed by Black women in academia.

A further study gives voice to young Black males, a group frequently stigmatized and subjected to pejorative stereotyping, and explores how some turn around their school 'failure' to achieve success. Despite schooling difficulties, they demonstrate a determination to succeed. Resources such as family and community play a vital role.

Clearly then, young people and the Black community value educational success. We struggle, after school is over, to achieve academic success and wider societal goals.

The essence of my activist 'academic work' as described in this chapter is eloquently articulated by a participant in a recent study of Black academics (Wright *et al.*, 2018: 80):

> A sense of wanting to give back what I have been given (by my forebears) and learnt using knowledge and experience to change thinking and perceptions about the place of Black women as leaders, to support the younger Black generation and our children. I have a strong belief in our power to change and that our history of resilience and being resilient still shows this to be true. It also makes us a force to be reckoned with.

References

Bassel, L. and Emejulu, A. (2017) *Minority Women and Austerity: Survival and resistance in France and Britain*. Bristol: Policy Press.

Bryan, B., Dadzie, S. and Scafe, S. (1985) *The Heart of the Race: Black women's lives in Britain*. London: Virago.

Davis, A.Y. (1981) *Women, Race, and Class*. London: Women's Press.

Etienne, J. (2016) *Learning in Womanist Ways: Narratives of first generation African Caribbean women*. London: Trentham Books.

Hansard 'Windrush Debate', 18 May 2018, House of Commons. Online. https://tinyurl.com/y9rohqtv (accessed 10 December 2019).

Harding, D.J. (2010) *Living the Drama: Community, conflict, and culture among inner-city boys*. Chicago: University of Chicago Press.

Hill Collins, P. (2000) *Black Feminist Thought: Knowledge, consciousness, and the politics of empowerment*. 2nd ed. New York: Routledge.

hooks, b. (1989) *Talking Back: Thinking feminist, thinking black*. Boston: South End Press.

hooks, b. (1992) *Black Looks: Race and representation*. Boston: South End Press.

hooks, b. (1994) *Teaching to Transgress: Education as the practice of freedom*. New York: Routledge.

hooks, b. (1995) *Killing Rage: Ending racism*. New York: Henry Holt and Company.

hooks, b. (2003) *Teaching Community: A pedagogy of hope*. New York: Routledge.

Ladson-Billings, G. (2005) 'The evolving role of critical race theory in educational scholarship'. *Race Ethnicity and Education*, 8 (1), 115–19.

Lawrence, E. (1982) 'In the abundance of water the fool is thirsty: Sociology and black "pathology"'. In Centre for Contemporary Cultural Studies *The Empire Strikes Back: Race and racism in 70s Britain*. London: Hutchinson, 95–142.

Lorde, A. (1984) *Sister Outsider: Essays and speeches*. Trumansburg, NY: Crossing Press.

Mirza, H.S. (ed.) (1997) *Black British Feminism: A reader*. London: Routledge.

Motune, V. (2018) 'More BAME uni applications'. *The Voice*, 11 February. Online. https://tinyurl.com/tenfvu8 (accessed 10 December 2019).

NCES (National Center for Education Statistics) (2018) *The Condition of Education 2018* (NCES 2018-144). Washington, DC: US Department of Education. Online. https://nces.ed.gov/pubs2018/2018144.pdf (accessed 18 July 2018).

Perlow, O.N., Wheeler, D.I., Bethea, S.L. and Scott, B.M. (eds) (2018) *Black Women's Liberatory Pedagogies: Resistance, transformation, and healing within and beyond the academy*. Cham: Palgrave Macmillan.

Reynolds, T. (2008) *Ties That Bind: Families, social capital and Caribbean second-generation return migration* (Working Paper 46). Brighton: University of Sussex.

Shiner, M. and Modood, T. (2002) 'Help or hindrance? Higher education and the route to ethnic equality'. *British Journal of Sociology of Education*, 23 (2), 209–32.

Sian, K. (2017) 'Being black in a white world: Understanding racism in British universities'. *Papeles del CEIC: International Journal on Collective Identity Research*, 2, Article 176, 1–26. Online. https://tinyurl.com/qrd7w67 (accessed 5 December 2019).

Toone, A., Edgar, A.N. and Ford, K. (2017) '"She made angry black women something that people would want to be": *Lemonade* and black women as audiences and subjects'. *Participations: Journal of Audience and Reception Studies*, 14 (2), 203–25.

Walker, A. (1983) *In Search of Our Mothers' Gardens: Womanist prose*. San Diego: Harcourt Brace Jovanovich.

Wijeyesinghe, C.L. and Jones, S.R. (2013) 'Black college women and intersectionality: Examining and interweaving core concepts and themes'. In Strayhorn, T.L. (ed.) *Living at the Intersections: Social identities and black collegians*. Charlotte, NC: Information Age Publishing, 125–51.

Williams, B. (2017) 'Black women in social movements: 5 history-making activists you should celebrate this month'. *Essence*, 3 March. Online. https://tinyurl.com/smycew9 (accessed 10 December 2019).

Williams, P. (2018) 'Silenced and objectified: Black women in the US'. *Times Literary Supplement*, 5 January. Online. https://tinyurl.com/uewn2mr (accessed 10 December 2019).

Wright, C. (2005) 'Black educational experiences in Britain: Reflections on the global educational landscape'. In King, J.E. (ed.) *Black Education: A transformative research and action agenda for the new century*. Mahwah, NJ: Lawrence Erlbaum Associates.

Wright, C. (2013) 'Understanding black academic attainment: Policy and discourse, educational aspirations and resistance'. *Education Inquiry*, 4 (1), 87–102.

Wright, C. (2017) 'The body politic: The impact of everyday racism and sexism on black women's experiences in politics'. *Labour Briefing: Magazine of the Labour Briefing Co-operative*, March/April, 16–17.

Wright, C., Maylor, U. and Becker, S. (2016) 'Young black males: Resilience and the use of capital to transform school "failure"'. *Critical Studies in Education*, 57 (1), 21–34.

Wright, C., Maylor, U. and Watson, V. (2018) 'Black women academics and senior managers resisting gendered racism in British higher education institutions'. In Perlow, O.N., Wheeler, D.I., Bethea, S.L. and Scott, B.M. (eds) *Black Women's Liberatory Pedagogies: Resistance, transformation, and healing within and beyond the academy*. Cham: Palgrave Macmillan, 65–83.

Wright, C., Thompson, S. and Channer, Y. (2007) 'Out of place: Black women academics in British universities'. *Women's History Review*, 16 (2), 145–62.

Wright, C. and Weekes, D. (2003) 'Race and gender in the contestation and resistance of teacher authority and school sanctions: The case of African Caribbean pupils in England'. *Comparative Education Review*, 47 (1), 3–20.

Part Two

Intergenerational voices:
Black women respond to
crisis and black youth

Chapter 5

Black youth, loss of trust and the crisis of knife crime: Pursuing a Womanist strategy

Palmela Witter

This chapter focuses on the increasing number of deaths among black youth in Britain's cities from knife crime. It does not seek to put forward definitive answers but a view of the tragedy through the eyes of a black Womanist activist, and draws on black feminist epistemology in the work of hooks (2000) and Lorde (1981) as a political and theoretical frame to explore a possible role for Britain's struggling black voluntary sector. In exploring the issues, the chapter primarily focuses on London and examines what the UK media, police and others have described as an epidemic of incidents of knife crime now implicating all communities.

I discuss what I consider to be a necessary co-ordinated collectivism within black and ethnic minority communities if we are to help stem the rising tide of violence in the areas most affected. In arguing for a Womanist approach, I will specifically consider the role of the black voluntary community sector.

Womanist identity

'Sisterhood is still powerful' (hooks, 2000).

I begin by asking: Who am I? A black feminist? A community activist? A Womanist? I would not immediately have called myself a feminist. However, when I was asked a question relating to black women and the UK reggae music industry at a public book reading, the host announced '.... And now we have the feminist's voice ...' I was indignant and vehemently challenged the host for calling me a feminist. Me – a feminist? I didn't believe that I was. I certainly didn't see that as me.

However, I dare say that from some unconscious idea I dismissed the label because I equated 'feminist' with radical white female who was devoid of interest or understanding about my issues and those of the black community. However, when given the floor to respond, I was struck by a bolt of 'black feminist' enlightenment, and subsequently presented myself as a black feminist, a Womanist, simply by asking a question about black women in the UK reggae industry. I was unconsciously thinking from a black Womanist perspective, striving to challenge the many social injustices faced by the black community in society today due to racism, discrimination and inequalities in health, education, employment and the judicial system. I suddenly recognized myself for who I really was and what I stood for – a Womanist with a deep interest in her community.

In what follows, I discuss whether a necessary co-ordinated collectivism within the black and ethnic minority community can stem the rising tide of violence. I argue that it is time for a new Womanist approach because of the ineffectiveness of current government, local authority and mainstream voluntary sector strategies. I also specifically explore the role of the black voluntary sector in addressing this matter.

My earlier years as a youth worker, community development worker, parent worker and black mother and sister had equipped me well. Within every platform I operated in, the many opportunities I had when engaging with other black women and our community, sharing our stories of raising children, searching for advice about education, health and personal lives – connecting with each other and through our 'lived experiences' – all this was the activist platform in which we in the black community operated (Etienne, 2016). As a postgraduate, researcher and community activist, I believe I now have an opportunity to raise black Womanist consciousness around this issue.

Context

At the time of writing this chapter, 267 young black boys and girls have become both the 'visible' and 'invisible' statistics of UK knife and gun crime. Consequently, I focus not on the statistics (Allen and Audickas, 2018) or the root causes of knife crime, but on a possible way forward in reducing the number of incidents, beginning with the black community.

From the late 1990s into the early 2000s, my interest in the black and minority ethnic voluntary and community sector came about in two distinct ways. First, my early working experience as a local authority monitoring officer thrust me into the arena of community development, capacity building, fundraising and being the gatekeeper of local authority funds and grants to small and medium-sized local voluntary and community sector groups for services in health, social care, children and young people – many of them long established grassroots black and minority ethnic voluntary organizations. Having a good understanding of the interface and relationship between local authorities and voluntary sector community groups (Harris and Rochester, 2001), I undertook an MSc in voluntary and community sector studies with a focus on black and minority ethnic organizations.

What is the black voluntary sector?

The black and minority ethnic voluntary sector has existed since the early 1960s (Davis and Cooke, 2002). Although at that time it was not formally recognized as part of the voluntary sector, it emerged from the need to address and challenge the inequality and race discrimination faced by marginalized black communities. In this chapter I refer to the UK black minority ethnic voluntary sector as the 'black voluntary sector', that provided a range of culturally specific activities and resources to meet the ethnic, cultural or religious needs not provided by mainstream providers (Paxton *et al.*, 2005). There is no one definition to describe the UK black voluntary sector, which is fragmented (Ware, 2018) by its diversity of identity, ethnicity, income, characteristics and size, and is therefore very difficult to define.

The black voluntary sector cannot be defined by 'what it is' but only by what it does and the type of organization it constitutes (Voice4change, 2007). However, despite its unique characteristics, the black voluntary sector sits on the periphery of the wider UK voluntary and community sector. Consequently, although recognized as being unique and distinctive (McCabe *et al.*, 2010), it lacks a 'voice or any influence' so it struggles to be at the decision-making table and cannot change or influence policy. The 2010 austerity measures saw a significant decline in UK voluntary and community sector organizations (NCVO, 2014) and the number of grassroots black voluntary organizations is dwindling further. As commissioning and funding are reduced, it struggles to survive.

The black voluntary sector and crime

So what is the black voluntary sector doing about crime among black youth? Depending upon how one views it, it may appear that the black community is doing very little about this situation – the right hand not knowing what the left hand is doing. In my earlier postgraduate research I found that the lack of statistics left gaps in the information available on models of good practice in black voluntary sector provision across London. From some case studies (NCIA, 2015) there is some evidence of exemplary work but organizations are spread too thinly across London and the threads that link them are weak and not well mapped.

Trying to establish what the black voluntary sector is doing about crime among black youth therefore proved challenging. Because the black voluntary sector is so fragmented by its diversity, size and type of service delivered, it's difficult to accurately capture local and regional initiatives. A snapshot might show women's and girls' groups, black and minority ethnic refugee groups, mental health projects, black men and boys' groups and black churches. Prominent London-based organizations include:

- Southall Black Sisters (southallblacksisters.org.uk). Established in 1979, it provides support, advice and guidance to women of black and Asian descent on domestic violence and honour marriages
- Imkaan (Imkaan.org.uk) is a second-tier black organization dealing with violence against black women and girls
- Black Training and Enterprise Group's (BTEG.org.uk) Routes to Success project, delivers training, role models, advice, support, access to employment and volunteers
- 100 Black Men (100bml.org) was established in 2001 and provides mentoring programmes, training, education and training for boys and men aged 11–25
- Damilola Taylor Trust – mentoring and development programmes, leadership and conflict resolution

Although they are not recognized as voluntary groups, I also include:

- The black churches and faith groups whose facilities are used by black community groups to provide safe havens for young people to avoid violence on the streets.

Targeting black youth violence: Media, funding and preventative strategies

The relentless stream of news in 2018 reporting young black boys being stabbed to death (Traynor, 2018) in chiefly gang-related incidents (Scott, 2018) is shocking, and the age of the victims worrying. My 10-year-old grandson informed me that he had attended a 'Stay Safe at School and on the Streets' event at his South London primary school. This prompted me to explore how Womanist strategies could help support black voluntary organizations in addressing this crisis.

Currently, the office of the Mayor of London has contributed some £1.4 million (Mayor of London, 2017), under the 2017 Knife Crime Strategy (www.gla.gov.uk), to 34 local projects to deliver a range of innovative programmes and strategies to help combat knife crime. The Mayor has contributed a further £1.5 million under his Anti-Knife Crime initiative to some 43 local projects in Lambeth, Southwark, Newham, Waltham Forest, Merton, Haringey, Croydon, and Hammersmith and Fulham. This will fund activities ranging from mentoring to martial arts, boxing and sports coaching. From a purely altruistic perspective, I understand the need for financial support to enable these types of projects to meet a perceived need. But I struggle to see how local, piecemeal, one-off preventative strategies are going to solve the problem of knife crime. The issues around this crisis are far more deep-rooted, multi-layered and driven by social, economic and political factors (Youth and Policy, 2017) – not forgetting the overriding lack of trust the black community feels towards the police. I see no joined-up working; these initiatives all appear to be operating in silos.

The state, local authorities and mainstream voluntary sector have still not managed to reduce the murder rate, not even through work with the black community. New answers to the problem have been or are being developed largely without community consultation. The Scottish Violence Reduction Unit is a national centre of expertise in tackling violence, working in partnership with Police Scotland and the Scottish government to prevent violence wherever it is found, be it in the streets, classrooms, home or work places. They have adopted a public health approach that treats violence as a disease and seeks to diagnose and analyse the root causes by working locally and in hospital emergency rooms to connect and engage with patients affected by violence. Interestingly, this approach appears to be working.

Strategies for the black voluntary sector

The black voluntary sector needs to identify meaningful ways of filling existing gaps and identifying innovative strategies and a plan of action that may need to be radical. A radical approach is called for – a culturally specific strategy owned and recognized by the black community. Such culturally specific strategies would involve black expertise at every stage of discussion, presenting knowledge and evidence of our needs, interests, the impact of racism, and promoting the views of the black community. The current strategies in London have some impact but these are mainly one-off gains. We need locally and culturally specific strategies that could be adapted and replicated UK wide.

Involving black mothers and drawing on their lived experience points to a way forward. An innovative strategy that engages in this way could be developed for each of the 33 London boroughs that have a crime prevention strategy board. The leading black voluntary organization in each borough could network with its neighbouring borough to pool resources, knowledge and experience. Each borough could involve a black mother as a representative from a local activist group in the community. Which black voluntary organization is best placed to sit at this table?

Yes, I can already hear voices of dissent – why one organization and not another? We can spend a lot of time focusing on why things don't happen – but we have to start somewhere. And these black mothers have immense experience and knowledge to offer, as well as being grounded in their neighbourhoods.

The black voluntary sector can also be instrumental in orchestrating local campaigns and community engagement initiatives, and in liaising with schools, police and other stakeholders, GPs and health providers. I'm not saying that such networks aren't already in place in *some* boroughs. But that is the issue: they may be operational in some boroughs but they need to function well in all of them, and adapt according to local and regional demographics. The black voluntary sector could be instrumental – working as a pan-London community collective, building upon their collaborative links with community activists to combat knife crime.

Many people highlight the lack of father figures for young black boys but few have sought the views of black women as to whether this is a contributing factor. The result has been to pathologize the young people involved in crime and the victims. Where is the drive to amplify black women's voices (Hayes, 2016) for informing and making decisions in the black voluntary sector as we attempt to find solutions?

Black women's resilience: A Womanist strategy

My argument is that black women in the voluntary sector must be heard if we are to move forward. Black women play an essential role in delivering Womanist strategies to support black communities at this time of rising youth violence. A Womanist strategy that is immersed in education and an ethic of care places black women at the centre of the discussion as they work alongside fathers, schools and services in an effort to bring local communities together to effect change. These women can be found in matriarchal learning hubs (Etienne, 2016), in community settings, where they locate their learning and experience in the heart of their communities, and together develop skills for active citizenship.

There is much to be said for the many black women who, when facing hardship and despair, show such strength and resilience (Hill Collins, 1990; Byrd *et al.*, 2009). Their strong voices shine through and become a force to be reckoned with. Black Womanist activists need to reach out to the many mothers who demand that something be done about the appalling rise in the number of young black lives lost to knife crime.

However, the UK political arena is not empathically hospitable. Neither is it geared to deal with the emotional, personal, heartfelt voices of victims, especially not those of the black community. The media coverage encourages an 'othering', a voyeurism or simply a statistical distance. It has become incumbent upon those within the black voluntary sector to make space to step up and actively address the reality of what is going on within our community. This is key, and it is pivotal to the possible resolution of an ongoing tragedy. In the words of Kimberlé Williams Crenshaw:

> it's not about supplication, it's about power. It's not about asking, it's about demanding. It's not about convincing those who are currently in power; it's about changing the very face of power itself. (Crenshaw, 1995)

Yet we hear little about female community-led interventions regarding this issue of life and death. As the primary nurturers of young men, why are women not put up-front-and-centre in working towards any solutions? We have all the authority structures to involve the people at the heart of the issues but apparently fail to put their knowledge and experience to use.

The activism of black women is entrenched in the fabric of what is termed a 'black issue', a 'black problem that has greater societal impact' – predominantly affecting the black community. Nayak (2015: 8) referring to the pertinence of Lorde's work, highlights the ways black activism, race and social change are interlinked, and argues:

> Black women and our children know the fabric of our lives is stitched with violence and with hatred, that there is no rest ... for us, increasingly, violence weaves through the daily tissues of our living – in the supermarket, in the classroom, in the elevator, in the clinic and the schoolyard, from the plumber, the baker, the saleswoman, the bus driver, the bank teller, the waitress who does not serve us. (Nayak, 2015: 8)

Nayak vividly describes how black women have lived the multi-faceted experiences of knife crime and it may be no surprise that black problems have received so little attention from predominantly white power holders. For the lived experiences of black women to be heard, we need to claim the centre ground and frame the analysis – we need to be at the head of the policy-development table.

A new Womanist lens of enlightenment means looking at the shared and lived experiences among the 'sisterhood' (hooks, 2000) in the form of bereaved parents or parents of perpetrators, victims, siblings, and the knowledge of wider community activists. As black women we can talk about our identity, our sameness, our uniqueness, our gender, our race, culture and the disadvantages we face across many social spheres. But it is that lived experience that we share as a collective – gender and culturally specific but also as a black person – the intersectionality described by Crenshaw *et al.* (1995) – and it is this collectivism that forms a unique foundation upon which black organizations can strive. The need to bring about change is the driving force that keeps us going, to try and right the injustices we face still.

A crisis in our community

How many more young people, have to die, be injured or maimed? How many more mothers have to cry?:

> When we speak we are afraid our words will not be heard or welcomed. But when we are silent, we are still afraid. So it is better to speak. (Lorde, 1984)

When my 10-year-old grandson told me about the 'Stay Safe at School and on the Streets' event at his primary school, I wondered why I was so shocked, even though there were so many media reports about knife and gun crime across the UK. My shock has propelled me to try to position myself more deeply in the community, to explore what is really going on and how the black voluntary sector is responding.

I awoke the next morning to the BBC news report that another young black boy, aged 14, was found stabbed and was fighting for his life in a London hospital. Yet another statistic. Although this is hard to hear first thing in the morning, I had heard it all before and, dare I say, had become somewhat de-sensitized. Why should yet another senseless death fail to shock me much anymore? Is it because we have 'normalized' this act of depravity?

The loss of trust among black youth

It is reported that the police's strategy of intelligence-led policing, stop and search, joint enterprise and the Police's Trident Matrix are safe, reliable sound strategies to address, challenge and even end the rise of incidents of knife and gun crime. But the statistics say otherwise: these strategies have tended to intensify black youth's fear and mistrust of the police. Asked why they carry weapons, young people say that it is for protection; they feel they're not safe on the streets and have to carry a weapon to protect themselves (Gunter, 2017). From her research within youth projects, Milbourne (2013) argues that 'in rapidly changing situations the security of shared values is interrupted, producing a precarious environment for trust'

(2013: 105) so that already strained relationships between the police and young black men break down more readily.

Closer to home

So when I ask myself what is going on with our young black men and boys who become victims and perpetrators of knife, gun and gang crime, I am not alone. The question is constantly discussed by mothers, fathers, brothers, sisters, aunts and uncles in the community. It has been on the agenda of the British government, the Mayor of London, the Home Office, schools, church and faith groups, academics and the media. Although the focus of this chapter mainly pertains to young black boys within our community, I don't forget the young black girls who are also involved in knife and gun crime, and gang culture, or who are victims of gang rape and human trafficking.

The stabbings, deaths, and impact on the black community are portrayed on the TV and news media as though they are distant events (Pickard, 2009). And because they are presented as being at arm's length, they don't quite affect us personally. So when my neighbour's 15-year-old son was a victim of knife crime just around the corner from where I live, I was overcome with shock, horror and despair – it suddenly became too close for comfort; emotionally real. It could have been one of my grandchildren. And what about the child's family? This was when I said, 'this is enough'. Along with a few neighbours, we rallied the local community, organized a series of meetings with the community's children and young people, the local authority, schools, police and other local stakeholders, to ask questions about the safety of the area, the residents' fears, and police engagement, support and advice.

It is understandably shocking to learn that after the recent stabbing of a 14-year-old in London, a dozen mobiles were found in his bedroom. But should it be the parent's responsibility to know what the child has in his room? Do we as black parents really know what our children are up to? This speaks to the heart of the problem: that the blame is frequently individualized to families when, at the root, there are few youth workers or social centres left, that social policies have been progressively restricting young people's hopes of a good future, be it through access to educational success, jobs, employment or housing.

The voice of the black voluntary sector needs to be heard especially in relation to the social pandemic of knife and gun crime affecting the black community. Because both victim and perpetrator of this type of violence are predominantly black, it is hard not to conclude that the issue has been poorly addressed by the politicians who cannot identify with the problem.

How much do race, institutional racism, and discrimination shape both the rhetoric and the strategies (Williams and Clarke, 2016)?

What role can the VCS play?

The black voluntary and community sector has an extremely important role in looking at strategies to deal with this crisis. The sector has been at the forefront of challenging societal issues since the late 1970s, seeking to address more culturally specific services and support. However, black voluntary organizations are often seen as a 'fourth' sector, sitting on the periphery or outside the UK mainstream voluntary organizations (Ware, 2013), with little or no mainstream voice. Statistically, with only 5,000 black voluntary organizations out of some 1.5m voluntary bodies all across the UK, the picture is depressing and it is not surprising there is such an uphill challenge.

Black women and leadership in the VCS

One should not forget that black community activists of yesteryear were not only visible but had a vibrant and influential voice, perhaps because the issues of race, discrimination, exclusion and exploitation were higher on the political agenda in the 1970s, 80s and early 90s. From the 1960s to the 1980s prominent black activists such as Claudia Jones, Olive Morris, Bernie Grant, Darcus Howe and Linda Bellos constituted a significant presence, making changes to political and policy expectations and driving race relations legislation. All of them formidable black activists, they were recognizable, credible, influential, and prepared to stand up and make their voices heard.

Yet I ask you, the reader, who in your local community can you identify as someone of influence who can represent the black community now, at this crucial time? Who are the prominent black community activists of today? Little wonder that over the last 10 years the issue of race has become diluted, devalued and subsumed into one of the nine protected categories under the UK Equality Act 2010.

Look at the statistics showing the number of black women in leadership roles across the black voluntary sector. According to ACEVO (2017) of the 58 per cent of female charity CEOs in the UK voluntary community sector, only 3 per cent are from black and Asian backgrounds. If we break the figures down further, of the 540 CEOs within third-sector organizations, only 16 are of black or Asian descent. And since 2010 a combination of austerity, co-production, contracting and commissioning of local authority services has driven this figure still lower. The black voluntary sector is small – almost invisible – and now sits apart from the larger UK voluntary sector. And within that space it has little or no power, and little influence. Yet against this and against the backdrop of institutional racism, years of austerity and funding restrictions, the few remaining black voluntary sector organizations remain resilient in times of crisis (Witter, 2017). Black community activism has to be revived.

The role of black women activists

The voices of black women, many of them mothers, are critical to the current debate on knife crime because they speak with a voice that is rich with experience, that is raw, emotional, personal and powerful.

The black Womanist has two distinct voices. The first is concerned with questioning the gains that they have made on a black feminist agenda. The second, about addressing the racism and social inequalities that they face daily as members of the black community, is the voice that is needed. It may be time to organize differently as a collective, drawing on our strengths as black Womanist activists, and talking with the youngsters on the frontline. Current initiatives like those being promoted by the police and the Mayor of London don't appear to be reducing knife and gun crime overall. They are mainly piecemeal, one-off and based in specific localities, and they're heavily dependent on government funding. If the young people have creative ideas about how to prevent further tragedies we need to be listening to them and their sisters, mothers, aunts and grandmothers. Young people are the ones who have first-hand knowledge of the issues surrounding this violence and may have ideas about what could put a stop to it.

What black women activists in black VCSs can do

To create a platform for change I am calling for the creation of a Black Womanist forum across the black voluntary sector to work with schools, excluded pupil units, youth clubs and other organizations. This could be developed by black women at local borough levels and form part of the transformation of the black voluntary sector.

While the uncertainty of Brexit remains as we move into 2020, the promised easing of austerity offers an opportunity to take stock of how the black voluntary sector could be transformative. Let's avoid re-inventing the wheel but use the one we have. Let's learn from the older black women, the 'first generation', who migrated from the West Indies during the 1950s and 1960s. Those formidable women had to endure blatant racism, discrimination and prejudice yet, as Etienne (2016: 46) relates, their level of activism was born out of their collectivism, their shared lived experiences:

black women's desire to voice their experience and collectively organize themselves is articulated through ... Motherhood and family, education, employment and community activism.

Now is the time for the second generation of UK black women take a leaf out of the book of the first. Their narratives hold valuable lessons for the present crisis. We need an arena for critical learning and an opportunity to identify collective Womanist spaces and to build an influential platform for meaningful dialogue with black young people and collaborative community action.

Conclusion

I don't pretend to have the answers for ending the violence before another black mother must deal with the death of her son or daughter from knife crime. But the destruction of the young generation cannot continue. Black Womanist activists must lead from the front – coming together as a collective to join forces, stand up and make our voices heard. There are no clear answers or solutions, but we cannot continue to sit by. The challenge for black voluntary organizations is to change how they are viewed by mainstream society so they are recognized as a viable entity with an influential voice that is able to operate strategically.

I have sought to highlight the value of the black voluntary sector in remaining resilient and active in times of challenge. It is time to recognize what it can do now and in the future, given greater resources. Money doesn't solve all problems, however; it is group action that creates change. Black voluntary organizations underpinned by their communities are best placed to deal with the knife crime crisis. I've suggested that a Womanist voluntary sector forum be made part of the black voluntary sector. It will be greatly strengthened by the women's experiences, knowledge and the survival tools honed by our mothers.

Many black mothers are coming together to fight against knife crime in the black community. Their trauma over the loss of a child is told and heard within the black community, but outside it it is only another statistic. Black Womanist voices must become *formally* part of the solution.

References

Allen, G. and Audickas, L. (2018) *Knife Crime in England and Wales* (House of Commons Library Briefing Paper SN4304). London: House of Commons Library. Online. https://tinyurl.com/vf38uov (accessed 30 January 2020).

Byrd, R.P., Betsch Cole, J. and Guy-Sheftall, B. (eds) (2009) *I Am Your Sister: Collected and unpublished writings of Audre Lorde*. New York: Oxford University Press.

Crenshaw, K.W. (1995) 'Mapping the margins: Intersectionality, identity politics, and violence against women of color'. In Crenshaw, K., Gotanda, N., Peller, G. and Thomas, K. (eds) *Critical Race Theory: The key writings that formed the movement*. New York: New Press, 357–83.

Crenshaw, K., Gotanda, N., Peller, G. and Thomas, K. (eds) (1995) *Critical Race Theory: The key writings that formed the movement*. New York: New Press.

Davis, S. and Cooke, V. (2002) *The Role of Black Women's Voluntary Sector Organisations*. York: Joseph Rowntree Foundation.

Etienne, J. (2016) *Learning in Womanist Ways: Narratives of first-generation African Caribbean women*. London: Trentham Books.

Gunter, A. (2017) *Race, Gangs and Youth Violence: Policy, prevention and policing*. Bristol: Policy Press.

Harris, M. and Rochester, C. (2001) *Voluntary Organisations and Social Policy in Britain: Perspectives on change and choice*. Basingstoke: Palgrave.

Hayes, V. (2016) 'Who will protect black women's interests when their organisations are gone?'. *Race Matters*, 13 November. Online. https://tinyurl.com/qlabj6p (accessed 10 December 2019).

Hill Collins, P. (1990) *Black Feminist Thought: Knowledge, consciousness, and the politics of empowerment*. Boston: Unwin Hyman.

hooks, b. (2000) 'Sisterhood is still powerful'. In hooks, b. *Feminism is for Everybody: Passionate politics*. London: Pluto Press, 13–18.

Lorde, A. (1981) 'The master's tools will never dismantle the master's house'. In Moraga, C. and Anzaldúa, G. (eds) *This Bridge Called My Back: Writings by Radical Women of Color*. Watertown, MA: Persephone Press; 4th ed. Albany: SUNY Press, 2015.

Mayor of London (2017) *The London Knife Crime Strategy*. London: Greater London Authority.

McCabe, A., Phillimore, J. and Mayblin, L. (2010) '"Below the Radar" Activities and Organisations in the Third Sector' (Third Sector Research Centre Working Paper 29). Online. www.birmingham.ac.uk/generic/tsrc/documents/tsrc/working-papers/working-paper-29.pdf (accessed 11 December 2019).

Milbourne, L. (2013) *Voluntary Sector in Transition: Hard times or new opportunities?* Bristol: Policy Press.

Nayak, S. (2015) *Race, Gender and the Activism of Black Feminist Theory: Working with Audre Lorde*. London: Routledge.

NCIA (2015) *Fight or Fright: Voluntary services in 2015* (NCIA Inquiry into the Future of Voluntary Services, Summary and Discussion of the Inquiry Findings). London: National Coalition for Independent Action Online. www.independentaction.net/wp-content/uploads/2015/02/NCIA-Inquiry-summary-report-final.pdf (accessed December 2019).

NCVO (2014) *UK Civil Society Almanac 2014*. London. National Council for Voluntary Organisations. Online. https://tinyurl.com/y84hlmyn (Accessed 5 June 2020).

Pickard, S. (2009) 'Blade Britain and broken Britain: Knife crime among young people in Great Britain today'. *Revue Française de Civilisation Britannique*, 15 (3), 65–78.

Scott, S. (2018) *The War on Gangs or a Racialised War on Working Class Black Youths*. London: Monitoring Group.

Traynor, P. (2018) 'Knife crime: I spoke to young people who carry blades – and they want to stop the violence'. *The Conversation*, 21 June. Online. https://tinyurl.com/y8yo5x67 (accessed 6 December 2019).

Voice4Change England (2007) *Bridge the Gap: What is known about the BME third sector in England*. London: Voice4Change England.

Ware, P. (2013) *"Very Small, Very Quiet, a Whisper...": Black and minority ethnic groups: Voice and influence* (Working Paper 103). Birmingham: Third Sector Research Centre.

Ware, P. (2018) *"Walking on Treacle...": Black and minority ethnic experiences of community capacity building* (Briefing Paper 141). Birmingham: Third Sector Research Centre.

Williams, P. and Clarke, B. (2016) *Dangerous Associations: Joint enterprise, gangs and racism: An analysis of the processes of criminalisation of black, Asian and minority ethnic individuals*. London: Centre for Crime and Justice Studies.

Witter, P. (2017) 'Marginalizing diverse voices? Working with minority interests against the tide of mainstreaming'. In Milbourne, L. and Murray, U. (eds) *Civil Society Organizations in Turbulent Times: A gilded web?*, 83–101. London: Trentham Books.

Youth and Policy (2017) 'Youth and Policy: The final issue? Towards a new format'. *Youth and Policy*, 116. Online. www.youthandpolicy.org/y-and-p-archive/issue-116/ (accessed 11 December 2019).

Chapter 6

Drill music, violence and criminalization: Gendered platforms for resistance

Jan Etienne and Ezimma Chigbo

If everything was sweet and flowers were growing and it was sunny every day, and then this music we're making came out of nowhere, I could understand why people might have a problem. They don't like it because we're speaking the truth. (Rapper Skengo)

Introduction

The relationship between drill music and youth violence is attracting attention, following a spike in youth killings. London's murder rate in 2018 was reported to be higher than that of New York City. Metropolitan Police Commissioner, Cressida Dick has argued that drill music is inciting violence among young people, calling for more intense scrutiny around its content and production. As a result more than 30 music videos were removed from YouTube in the first months of 2019.

In this chapter, we adopt a conversational, reflective approach as I engage in conversation with a black woman in her twenties, a youth practitioner, undergraduate student, writer and podcaster on her perspective on drill music and its association with increasing crime and violence. What impact does she think it is having on the lives of black youth in Britain?

The chapter begins with one of her blog posts (Chigbo, 2018a), which presents a reaction to a 'self-proclaimed criminal's' incarceration, and reveals the background to her interest in the topic and her personal involvement. The conversation that follows, on the history of drill, offers insights into the messages in the lyrics and their likely impact on young black men. Ezimma speaks about the participation of black women in the drill scene. Her second blog post (Chigbo, 2018b) discusses the involvement of young black women and the future of drill in the context of rising crime.

Ezimma's blog post 1 begins:

J Hus says in his Instagram:

'I'm tired of making the same mistakes ... every two years I have gone back to jail. The people that are gonna judge me know nothing about my circumstances/never experienced a sprinkle of the madness we have to go through.'

I've been thinking about why I'm saddened that a man who broke the law may have to face the consequences of his actions. I recently read on Twitter that J Hus will be going back to prison because a knife was found in the car he was travelling in. My immediate reaction was shock, followed by a familiar sadness. I am sad because as a youth practitioner, as a sister, as a black woman, and as someone that has been personally affected by street violence, I have grown to understand the various factors that may have contributed to J Hus risking his freedom in this way.

This isn't about knives. This is about a specific type of violence and the mind-set behind it for victims and perpetrators. It is time we considered that the lines between these two positions are blurred – notwithstanding the black and white picture being painted by mainstream media.

Some will question my response to this news. I've heard J Hus described as a 'self-proclaimed criminal' and because I have worked tirelessly to support young people and steer them away from choosing violence, some people will expect me to join them in condemning Hus. I understand this but I believe it oversimplifies a complex situation.

Many people are operating on the assumption that economic mobility directly translates to social mobility. This is not true. Of course, having more money exposes J Hus to more options regarding lifestyle but it is lazy to conflate wealth and fame with social mobility, the two are interlinked but not the same. Wealth and fame do not erase people's experiences, histories, beliefs, norms or values. J Hus is 23 years old. In 2015, aged 20, and in the infancy of his career, he was stabbed five times. As someone who grew up in and around street violence myself, I understand the trauma contained in Hus's story, therefore judgement is not my first reaction when I consider his decision to carry a knife.

When I was 17 I was beaten up by a group of boys and girls and stabbed in the head with a metal object. This experience and the months that followed plunged me to a unique darkness. I was paralysed with rage, fear and paranoia. There were days when I was consumed by thoughts of revenge, and days where I felt afraid to leave my house. After some weeks on this emotional rollercoaster I reached my breaking point and planned a violent retaliation – literally plotting and plotting.

My memory of how liberated I felt by my decision to react violently informs the empathy I offer J Hus when I think about the conditions leading to his arrest. Thoughts of avenging those who'd wronged me was the beginning of my process of accepting what had happened. My decision to retaliate allowed me to regain power and protect myself from future attacks that I had spent weeks in my bedroom hypothesizing. Thankfully, my elaborate plans for revenge did not pan out the way I imagined and circumstances spared me from myself. If things had gone even slightly differently, I would be telling a different story.

Through my work I can now name this as a classic case of trauma re-enactment. Determined to conquer the emotions I was experiencing, confronting the situation felt like the only solution, and violence was the form of confrontation that I knew. My environment had taught me that retaliation would free me of the fear that haunted me. Risking my life and freedom for this seemed inconsequential in comparison.

This may explain why J Hus went to Westfield and not some other shopping mall. Unfortunately, running from danger is seldom an option. Trauma has a knock-on effect that inevitably leaks out into the decisions people make. Wealth and fame can't magically erase this programming. This doesn't excuse violence, but it does highlight the vital need to support people living with trauma so they can alter the way they view and handle conflict.

This need extends to black women as well as young black men. For every black man that's imprisoned or killed, there are black women left behind to pick up the pieces. When a member of our community is a victim of street violence, the first to respond are black women. There is perpetual labour for black women because of this violence that has infected our communities, and this labour has not been sufficiently examined.

My emotional reaction to the news about Hus is symbolic of a wider discussion about the role that black women play. Black women are the backbone of our communities. Although it is usually men who are positioned at the centre of discussions on street violence, black women have a unique and inescapable relationship to the issue.

Young women's involvement in street violence is starting to be picked up by services. However, in their 2014 report on *Girls and Gangs,* the Centre for Social Justice asserts that 'the data on girls and young women is unreliable and too little is known about the reality of gang life for them'. Moreover, when women are victims of street violence, this is not always reported in the media although black women are also being stabbed, beaten up and shot. I personally have worked with a number of these women, and their stories are not told.

I haven't seen an adequate response by services to support women affected by street violence. Within the few services that do respond, women are too often treated as victims, with interventions that don't address the nuanced nature of their relationship with street violence. This is not good enough and we need to do more.

———

Jan: So what is it about the lyrics in drill music that is said to incite violence?

Ezimma: For this discussion to be meaningful it is important to acknowledge the violent culture that accompanies the art of drill music, and also the impact it may have on impressionable youth.

[What] if a young man raps 'I put rambo blades in chests, I put flick knives straight in necks. With a wap I'll aim for your head. If you see me you're looking at death.' I think it is important to first engage with the context of these lyrics and address the social factors that enable such lyrics to be created. And, we must remember that this is comparable to the response to gangsta rap in the 1990s and grime in the early 2000s. Both genres were criticized for inciting violence, yet both have now been accepted into mainstream popular culture.

Jan: How does this sit with the young people you work with?

Ezimma: Young people I've worked with have different opinions on the impact of drill on violence in Britain. It is imperative that spaces are made for these voices to be heard. For many of them, drill is the only viable pass for social and economic mobility.

Jan: What is your view on drill music and its association with the racialized element of youth violence?

Ezimma: It's difficult to ignore the racialized element of the drill conversation. There's something to be said about the wider narrative of how black youth around the world have been criminalized and feared without probable cause. In my view, the fact that it is predominantly black youth producing this music partly explains the extremity of the government's response. In fact, the consumers of drill are not exclusively black youth – or youth in general. Addressing black youth as either victims or perpetrators with nothing in between is part of the problem – it's an attempt to silence those brave enough to document the dire environments in which they live.

Jan: Fatsis (2019) refers to the policing of drill as 'an expression of the discriminatory politics that neoliberal economics facilitates in order to exclude those who the state deems undesirable or undeserving of its protection'. Are there other implications?

Ezimma: I think it raises concerns about the responsibility of those within the music industry who profit from the production of this music and also white middle-class beneficiaries who continue to fund the music. If the consensus is that young people should be penalized for producing this style of music, then surely similar sanctions should be put in place for anyone benefiting from its production? Why are record labels, radio stations and music channels being allowed to freely profit from drill music if it is causing the increase in killings among British youth? Although this will not be the first time the impact of music on society has been scrutinized in this way.

Jan: Can you elaborate on that?

Ezimma: There's a notable pattern of Black music in Britain facing resistance before it is accepted in the mainstream. Before drill, similar discussions were had about grime music. I've heard that popular grime artists such as So Solid Crew, Kano, Giggs and Skepta have all had performances prevented by law from being put on, for fear that they would incite violence.

Jan: So what do you make of the current discussion on drill music?

Ezimma: This discussion taking place among policy-makers, law enforcement and communities has been framed around the relationship between drill and youth violence. We know that black youth in London are disproportionately affected by youth violence and the numbers continue to rise. We are also over-represented in the prison population and we are told that drill music has a part to play here. But I wouldn't entirely agree with everything the policymakers and the like have said. It is important to recognize that drill is not exclusively produced and consumed by black youth. Although the drill scene in the UK and abroad is overwhelmingly comprised of black youth and plays a noteworthy role in contemporary Black British culture (Thompson, 2014).

Jan: What can you tell me about the discussions on Drill in Britain?

Ezimma: An increase in stabbings and other violent crimes has brought the drill conversation to the mainstream, though drill has been part of underground youth culture in Britain for some years now. Drill was birthed in Chicago and is considered a subgenre of trap-rap and hip-hop. Chicago is known for its high levels of poverty and gang culture linked to race, deprivation and territory.

Jan: What do you think is the relationship between drill music and gang culture?

Ezimma: I can't ignore the fact that from its inception, drill has been entwined with gang culture. Drill artists are usually affiliated with specific groups or geographical locations and their lyrics are typically descriptive of violence committed against enemies from rival territories. Chicago rappers used localized vernacular coupled with harsh beats to portray the harshness of their environments and some of the dire circumstances they've faced. Simple sentence structures and flows are used within drill to communicate extreme violence that's already occurred or violence artists are claiming they hope to inflict on their enemies. Artists such as King Louie and Chief Keef pioneered the sound and after an outbreak of self-recorded music videos, Chief Keef broke into the international market in 2012 before his incarceration.

Jan: How did drill find its way to the UK?

Ezimma: In the UK the music first found its way to south London with popular drill group 67 (pronounced six-seven) adopting the US style of rap but infusing it with London influences of grime and UK rap. Hailing from Brixton Hill, 67 rapped about similar themes explored by Chief Keef and King Louie but shone light on the London context. Brixton has historical significance for the black community and became home to many Caribbean settlers of the Windrush generation. Brixton has been a hub for black resistance dating back to before the 1981 race riots, so there is some irony in the fact that many of the grandchildren of these settlers are in a way, sort of disrupting today's society with this music.

Jan: And what of its reach in other areas?

Ezimma: The production of drill has since spread beyond south London to other marginalized communities around the UK. In London, popular drill artists and groups hail from Tottenham, Hackney and Ladbroke Grove, areas that have experienced historical racial tensions, high levels of street crime and concentrated social housing estates.

Social housing and drill music

Ezimma: Drill groups are usually comprised of young people who have all grown up in the same area. Poor social housing and deprivation are the conditions with which most drillers are forced to make something out of their dire situation. For many disenfranchised groups of young men in particular, drill is the soundtrack to local life (Thapar, 2018). Drill collectives are usually comprised of groups of young people from council estates they grew up on. Music videos are often recorded on these housing estates. These groups rap about experiences they face in their local communities, and they can use drill to taunt other young people from opposing areas. There is a territorial nature to the music and it's been known for groups to engage in conflict online with their enemies or 'opps'.

Jan: Do you see a link with social class here?

Ezimma: Yes, there is a clear correlation between the production of this style of music and working-class black communities. There is also a correlation between the issues raised within the genre and working-class black communities.

Jan: Researchers Pinkney and Robinson-Edwards recently pointed out that 'Gang research in the main is predicated on the notion that gangs are deviant products of social disorganization' (2018). What is your view?

Ezimma: Drill is an emotive genre of music, describing the hardships faced by many black youth – from poverty to racism, gang violence or family conflicts – drill uniquely maps the experiences of many black youths in their own words.

Drill music and the influence of social media

Jan: Urbanik and Haggerty (2018) observe that:

> These men are drawn to social media in part because they allow them to communicate with far-flung and potentially global audiences. However, the types of messages they post or in which they inadvertently appear can enhance their risk of victimization in their travels through the city.

Do you agree with them and to what extent has social media played a part in mainstreaming drill music?

Ezimma: Yes I agree with them and consider the quote an important one. A combination of factors enabled the transition from drill as an underground sound to a more mainstream, international trend. Yes, social media has played a major role in the mainstreaming of drill, the nature of drill's DIY approach means the internet and social media are a handy tool for sharing music videos on Snapchat, Instagram and other social media platforms. Artists use Snapchat and Instagram to promote themselves and their music. In their study on crime, rap music and social media conducted in one of Toronto's marginalized communities, Urbanik and Haggerty argued that conveying a message of strength in numbers signalled that a rapper, gang or neighbourhood was not easily intimidated, and that violence would be met with violence.

Jan: Social media is playing a significant role, would you say? And what are your thoughts on the risk of victimization – and violence?

Ezimma: Yes. Artists are able to monitor the movements of their rivals using social media. And as I pointed out earlier, music videos are also an integral part of the drill culture. Drillers have been criticized for flaunting weapons in their videos and portraying themselves in threatening ways. Drill music videos tend to feature large numbers of youths. This is something to consider when analysing the rise in violence in Britain. Social media plays a vital role within the drill scene. There is an undeniable relationship between the online personas of these musicians and their lives offline. Some would argue that for this reason the growing popularity of drill music is directly linked to spikes in violent crimes committed by young people.

Jan: Can we return your thoughts on youth practitioner and journalist Ciaran Thapar's views on drill?

Ezimma: Ciaran Thapar has reported extensively on the UK drill scene, referring to drill artists as 'local news reporters'. Thapar has consistently challenged the demonization of drill by mainstream media and policymakers, claiming that a number of social factors have contributed to the rise in youth violence.

Austerity and drill

Jan: Do you make any links between austerity and drill music?

Ezimma: Most certainly. The emergence of drill coincided with the Conservative government's austerity and in particular cuts in youth services, which culminated in the closure of youth clubs. In my view, analysing the impact of this music on society is as important as analysing the many other social factors that may have contributed to increased violence among black youth. I have already referred to the existing relationship between social housing, drill music and black youth violence. Cuts to public services directly affected the most marginalized communities in the UK.

> Drill artist AM is quick to add: I feel like if there were statistics on this, then we inspire more young people to start rapping than do violence ... People hear one thing and think that's all we're about. I might be thinking: 'Hold on. I can actually get somewhere with this, let me keep pushing and try and make something positive out of it.' But all a next man's hearing is: 'Thugs, thugs, thugs ...'. The media portray us as negative people who don't have dreams or ambition when really and truly everybody wants something in life.

Jan: This is powerful.

Ezimma: When lamenting the social conditions which pushed him towards producing drill, let me read to you what drill artist AM states:

> In a place where people have low incomes, where they are struggling, respect becomes the most important thing. People want respect, they crave it. It makes a lot of people do crazy things. I do the most I can for the people around me but I don't feel like I can stay. I want to prove I can break out of the system.

Ciaran Thapar describes this poignantly: 'Drill is this generation's furious response against the Conservative government's decimation of state support for the most vulnerable communities under austerity.

Black women and the UK drill scene

Jan: Can you now share with me your thoughts on black women's involvement in the UK drill scene?

Ezimma: Although generally drill is a male-dominated environment there are a number of upcoming female drillers in Britain. In my role as a youth practitioner I have worked mainly with young people who have had some level of involvement with the criminal justice system. I specialize in working with young women, an overwhelming majority of these women being black and mixed race. There is what I see as the sexualization of female drillers vs the 'masculine' presentation of female drillers. Young women in drill tend to fall into one or the other category.

Jan: Please elaborate?

Ezimma: Women are making and enjoying drill music alongside their male counterparts. Women are not always portrayed positively within drill. In her chapter 'Gangsta Culture – Sexism and Misogyny: Who Will Take The Rap?', bell hooks (1994) confronts the tension between negative portrayals of women in rap. She pointed out that the sexist, misogynistic, patriarchal ways of thinking and behaving that are glorified in gangsta rap are a reflection of the prevailing values in our society, values created and sustained by white supremacist capitalist patriarchy. I think this is relevant in the drill conversation too.

I have worked in settings where young women are producing drill songs with hyper sexualized lyrics. Although falling into the stereotypically oppressive narrative about young women in hip-hop, these women have used their agency to rap in this way. I have also worked with young women who have a somewhat therapeutic relationship with drill. Through their music they are able to talk openly about trauma and the emotions which accompany their adverse childhood experiences. Music serves as a tool to communicate their message, a message that they were either unwilling or unable to communicate outside of the medium of music.

Jan: So in what ways would you say young black women are implicated in the violence that's said to accompany drill?

Ezimma: Are we talking about drill, or are we talking about violence? I do not see the two as synonymous. If we're talking about violence then there has been an increase in young women being arrested and convicted for violent crimes. I would argue that for far too long young women have been known to deal with conflict in a way that is not overtly disruptive in society, and this trend is changing. A high percentage of women in the prison estate are there for violent crimes, often violent crimes committed against an intimate partner. The reaction to Tanesha Melbourne-Blake's murder in Tottenham last year demonstrates that British society is still shocked when young women are victims of this form of violence. Tanesha's gender disqualified her from the prototype of an expected victim of this type of crime. This shows that black women are to some degree still afforded the 'victim' narrative.

Young black women are not the main perpetrators of youth violence but we play a vital role in creating solutions for youth violence. We are often left to pick up the pieces when black men are arrested or killed. It is black women who are left to carry the burden.

Jan: Do you see black women in drill music getting their message across?

Ezimma: It's black men who are making the headlines although black women are directly and indirectly affected by youth violence. In my view, services are tailored towards the male experience. When black men are affected by high rates of crime and violence, this inevitably affects black women. In relation to drill, women have formed groups in Manchester in response to a recent murder case in which drill music was cited as the cause. These mothers created a platform for resistance and advocacy on behalf of the incarcerated young men.

Jan: What do you see as a way forward?

Ezimma: Before the question is posed on how to effectively deter young people from reacting to the violence they are exposed to through drill music, I have found that it is important to engage young people in these discussions regarding policy change. It is the only way they will be able to gain their buy-in when implementing relevant changes.

Jan: Do you blame the drill musicians for the violence?

Ezimma: No. It's important to address the conditions which created this culture in the first place (Bakkali, 2019). I think it is important to explore in more depth the conditions which enable this music to be produced as well as what it is about this music that is so attractive to young people from a range of socio-economic backgrounds. I have written elsewhere in my blogs that it is lazy to conflate wealth and fame with social mobility. In my view it is also lazy to address the negative outputs produced by young people without paying equal attention to the trauma being re-enacted in these songs and videos.

More visibility is needed for black women in the drill scene. Services on offer to young black women do not address their nuanced relationship with youth violence.

Jan: Would you recommend anything else?

Ezimma: More research needs to go into the conditions which enable these lyrics to be written and performed by British children all over the country. I do believe that there is a clear correlation between deprived communities and high rates of crime and violence among young people.

Jan: Do you see your blog posts inspiring others?

Ezimma: I hope my blog posts inspire other young black women to speak out in this way. I must say I have been inspired by other young black female writers and activists. I write how I feel and let the words speak for themselves. Anything I've ever written on the topic is heartfelt, honest and personal. I see my words as a small contribution to the black woman's wider narrative – playing my part to protest on a deeply challenging issue.

Jan: What is your experience of working with young women involved in producing drill music?

Ezimma: I've delivered a number of workshops with young women exploring the relationship between drill and youth violence.

Allow me to reflect on one such workshop in my blog:

> I was co-delivering a session at Raw Material studio with a small group of young women when I first came across this young woman who was adamant she wanted to pursue a career in music. The project gives young women aged 12–14 in Southwark space to explore conflict in their lives as well as the opportunity to learn about and express themselves through music.

> This young woman's confidence and determination both in and out of the booth was inspiring. She had with her a notebook filled with lyrics that she'd written, which she boasted about adding to daily. It was clear she'd prepared for this opportunity and seemed really excited to record her track. When the time came she already knew which instrumental she wanted to record her vocals over, and eagerly searched for it while the rest of us looked on in admiration and anticipation. It was no surprise to me when a drill beat burst through the speakers. I had not heard this particular beat before, but I was familiar with its sound, furthermore I was familiar with the emotions its sound invoked in me. My co-facilitator spoke briefly with the girls about the history of drill, mumble rap and other subgenres of hip-hop before the aforementioned young woman entered the booth to record.

> In all honesty, I don't think this aspiring young musician cared much for the history lesson. All she wanted was an opportunity to get in the booth and express herself. She could barely contain her excitement. It is unlikely that this group of young women are up to speed on the current debate around censoring drill music, and even if they are, it is even less likely that they care about what the media, police or politicians have to say on the matter. What was clear to me in this session was this young woman's need to be heard, her confidence to communicate a story and her genuine

faith that this form of communication would be a much-needed platform for social and economic mobility.

I am no expert on drill, but I have always viewed it as a political, provocative genre of music; a genre which articulates the intense levels of pain many young people live with. Drill lyrics can be hard to digest, they tend to be vulgar, laced in hyperbole and their intention is clearly to provoke a response or a reaction from listeners. I am well aware of how this combination of factors can fuel conflict among peer groups, prompting young people to react violently, but I believe strongly that censoring this form of expression is not the suitable answer to that problem.

For starters, if violence is the framework that young people have for managing conflict then violence will be the inevitable outcome whenever it arises, no matter what music is listened to. Moreover, censoring this form of expression in no way addresses some of the root causes behind these lyrics and the violence in this music has the potential to [afford] insight.

It would be naïve to ignore the negative messages behind most drill tracks or the way this may negatively impact young people's lives. However, it is important to understand that through this music young people are communicating something, not only to their peers but to all of society. As adults taking in the overtly violent lyrics and music videos being written, directed and performed by children and young adults all over the country – what message are we choosing to take from this? Is our role simply to silence these artists with some hope that the problems go away? Or do we have the capacity to meaningfully engage with the themes these artists are addressing? My view is that it is our responsibility to create safe spaces that allow young people to explore the themes this music promotes as well as spaces which support young people to develop skills to aid them to manage conflict better.

A number of young women I work with listen to drill. Drill music seems to have penetrated youth culture across the country, appealing to young people from a vast range of backgrounds. An experience not dissimilar to the impact hip-hop and grime music had on me and my peers when I was a teenager; or the impact jazz, rock, blues and most other forms of music had on generations before mine. Grime was so embedded in the culture of my youth that it was very difficult to analyse the music without noting its social impact. I vividly remember the way grime was framed in the media to be inciting violence among young people. I remember popular grime artists such as So Solid Crew, Giggs and J Hus being banned from performing their music in public arenas and I remember the message this relayed to me at the time – that stories from my community were not worth listening to.

Although this was the mainstream interpretation of grime, it was far from my personal experience of it. For me, grime music put words to so many of my experiences growing up as a working-class black girl in London. Grime made my reality visible to an audience who were ignorant of the world I and my friends manoeuvred, a world that was strikingly underrepresented in mainstream media. Grime highlighted that there was a community of people who had similar experiences to mine, who shared similar frustrations about structural forms of violence such as poverty and racism that I felt victim to. Grime artists made me feel that my story was valuable, that it was worth speaking about and listening to. Were there violent, misogynistic or problematic lyrics in grime? Yes. However, there was so much more to the music and to the culture than that.

Ezimma goes on to reflect more closely:

Over the weekend I spent some time with my brother discussing our shared love for grime. We spoke at length about the similarities between the ways the media and the police portrayed grime in our day to how drill is being discussed today. We spoke about what it meant to us to listen to Dizzee Rascal's Boy In da Corner for the first time and compared this to the pride we feel 15 years later watching A$AP Rocky's Praise the Lord video featuring Skepta. Grime continues to tell a story that I am familiar with, a story which may not be prim and proper but resembles my lived experience – a narrative which I believe is important enough to be told and to be heard.

Not everyone who listens to grime or drill music will be able to relate to it on a personal level but this does not mean that they are incapable of engaging with its themes. Young people, like the young woman described in this post, are using this music to relay their stories or the stories of others whom they usually exist in close proximity to. These stories can be challenging as they shine a light on some of the ugliest manifestations of deprivation in this country. I think it's time we had an honest discussion about potential solutions for the causes of these conditions as opposed to its effects.

Or, as Dizzee Rascal so eloquently put it, 'Got some mates that have been convicted, yeah, so what, it's the hand life dealt them, we weren't blessed with the system's TLC, government shoulda tried to help them.' (Leap Confronting Conflict).

Conclusion

Jan: And what role do you see your blog posts playing in the ongoing discussion on drill music?

Ezimma: A useful one, I hope. As a black woman in my twenties I feel it is important to have platforms like these, where we can air our views within a space that we own, that is not subjected to censorship in the true sense of the word. Here we are not told what to write and can get our messages across in our own way, put across things that are upsetting – issues that we want to share with others. I do see blogging as a type of activism because I am protesting about stuff that I feel is unjust and I am crying out for a platform for other black women to speak out on issues that affect us. My posts allow me space to express my anger and frustration to the world because black youth need to be able to do this. I wish more of us would do it. Previous research studies in this area of youth violence and gangs in urban areas expose the feelings of males (Bakkali, 2019), and our voices are rarely ever heard on a male-dominated topic such as drill music.

References

Bakkali, Y. (2019) 'Dying to live: Youth violence and the munpain'. *Sociological Review*, 67 (6), 1317–32.

Chigbo, E. (2018a) 'Is drill music contributing to the rise in violent crime? A young woman's worker speaks out'. Leap Confronting Conflict blog, 19 July. Online. https://tinyurl.com/uchg94u (accessed 9 December 2019).

Chigbo, E. (2018b) 'The cycle of street violence and its invisible victims'. *Black Ballad*, 10 August. Online. https://tinyurl.com/rvq7pdl (accessed 9 December 2019).

Fatsis, L. (2019) 'Policing the beats: The criminalisation of UK drill and grime music by the London Metropolitan Police'. *Sociological Review*, 67 (6), 1300–16.

hooks, b. (1994) 'Gangsta culture – sexism and misogyny: Who will take the rap?'. In hooks, b. *Outlaw Culture: Resisting representations*. New York: Routledge, 134–44.

Pinkney, C. and Robinson-Edwards, S. (2018) 'Gangs, music and the mediatisation of crime: Expressions, violations and validations'. *Safer Communities*, 17 (2), 103–18.

Thapar, C. (2018) 'What makes young people carry knives? It's not drill music for sure'. *The Guardian*, 23 February. Online. https://tinyurl.com/tklmnr8 (accessed 6 December 2019).

Thompson, C.H. (2014) 'Stuart Hall – Policing the Crisis'. Online. https://tinyurl.com/vla3h4w (accessed 9 December 2019).

Urbanik, M.-M. and Haggerty, K.D. (2018) '"#It's dangerous": The online world of drug dealers, rappers and the street code'. *British Journal of Criminology*, 58 (6), 1343–60.

Chapter 7

Pain, anger and youth resistance: Police racial awareness training and the contemplations of a black mother

Lurraine Jones

> *I am an Angry Black Woman. Unapologetically, rationally and rightfully so. I am blistering mad! I am frustrated and enraged! I am devastated, and my blood is boiling at a temperature so hot that I think my heart might stop beating at any given moment! I am so angry that I feel neurotic; it feels as if my mind has been lost to my critical eyes. (Griffin, 2012: 138)*

Introduction

This chapter analyses the complexities and conflicts of using an anti-racism employee training tool that is based on a racial epistemological framework that was created, built and shaped by institutional Whiteness. This human resources tool is used to practise police diversity training and therefore the policing of UK black communities. I contend that many inner-city UK police services have been historically shaped by institutionally racist policies and practices, and the interactions of rank and file police officers with black communities lead to the oft-quoted trope of black communities feeling 'over policed and under protected'. I explore my reactions as a black mother and engage with the challenges of racialization and the topic of 'race' in police diversity training and what I consider to be its unintended consequences for black youth.

Exploring emotions and rhetorical commitment to anti-racist practice

Diversity training is an organizational training tool, which teaches employees the business, legal and ethical reasons for inclusion, respect and cultural sensitivity in the workplace. My PhD research seeks to advance how racialized experience and positioning is manifested in diversity training within policing. 'Positioning' in this research context refers to majority white ethnic and black minority ethnic employees working within the predominantly white institution of policing. As Ahmed points out, 'if diversity is a way of viewing or even picturing an institution, then it might allow only *some* [emphasis added] things to come into view' (Ahmed 2012: 14).

What has come into view for me in my research is that as employees engage with and experience the topic of 'race' within diversity training, they will hold racialized, subjective views towards the materials and the trainer. Key elements of diversity training are personal growth and cultural awareness, and therefore I consider it crucial to understand and contribute to the contemporary racial politics discussion by exploring whether participants of this training do feel empowered and valued and empowered to value. Furthermore, I explore if and how they are able to align themselves with and beyond a rhetorical level of their employees' business, ethical and moral agenda. It is most certainly a positive aim within diversity training that participants are encouraged to 'confront' or 'address' their personal behaviour and attitudes to move towards anti-racist practices. It is also important to contemplate the following question: what might the consequences be within and for the organization in policing culturally diverse boroughs or communities if diversity training is not conducted?

As a black woman of mixed heritage, mother of four black children, and university lecturer involved in researching police diversity training, my chapter is influenced by these various identities. I set out to comprehend the nature of my pain and anger in facing the daily discriminatory treatment encountered by black youth in their interactions with white policing on UK streets.

In the context of the turbulence and antagonism directed towards the black community by white police since the 1950s, my research explores the anti-racism tool of diversity training. However, as a black woman, mother and educator, I recognize that such a tool is inevitably based on a racial epistemological framework created, built and shaped by institutional whiteness. My doctoral thesis positions itself within the intellectual spaces that black academics have created within white educational institutions to challenge white hegemonic discourses of racialization. I position myself as a black, female, senior lecturer in higher education with a desire to confront an unjust world that profoundly impacts on my life and my loved ones. My research is best described in terms of black feminist writer Toni Morrison's 1992 *Playing in the Dark: Whiteness and the Literary Imagination*. Morrison explains the invisibility of whiteness in literature as a fishbowl that contains fish and water. The fishbowl itself provides meaning as it contains the water and the fish, but one invariably focuses on the fish swimming in the water, and not the constraints of the fishbowl itself.

The murder of a black youth that changed a nation: 'Look – A Negro'

'"Dirty nigger!" Or simply, "Look, a Negro!".' (Fanon, 1986)

On 22 April 1993 in what has been called by the BBC documentary *The Murder That Changed a Nation* (2018), black teenager Stephen Lawrence was murdered at a bus stop in Eltham, south-east London in an unprovoked, racially motivated attack by five white male teenagers. Only two of the white perpetrators were convicted of Stephen's murder almost 20 years later, using DNA. A Scotland Yard spokesman recently stated:

> Despite previous public appeals, rigorous pursuit of all remaining lines of inquiry, numerous reviews and every possible advance in forensic techniques, the Met investigation team is now at a stage where without new information the investigation is unlikely to progress further, and this was explained to the family earlier this year. (Dodd, 2018)

Much has been written about Stephen's murder, and several commentators have referred to it as a watershed moment for UK policing. I remember watching the sad events unfold at the time I was the mother of two small children, and pregnant with twin boys due that June. As is often the case when such tragic events take place, one wonders what kind of world one is bringing children into, and I cried for Doreen and Neville Lawrence at the loss of their child. Perhaps because I was pregnant, I became very emotional about the state of a racist country where my own black children were most certainly going to be subject to racism at points in their lives, as myself, friends and families had been. My pain and anger grew as I followed the ensuing Metropolitan Police debacle of the initial investigation into Stephen's murder.

Black mother confronting whiteness

The three-part BBC documentary of 2018, *Stephen: The Murder That Changed a Nation*, detailed the events leading up to and following Stephen's murder. Although Neville Lawrence unquestionably sought justice for his son, it was clear that he had withdrawn into himself with grief. So it was a mother's enduring anger and tenacity that drove Doreen Lawrence to continue fighting publicly for over a decade to see her son's murderers convicted.

At Stephen's inquest, a stoic Baroness Lawrence stood up and read her speech:

> When my son was murdered, the police saw my son as a criminal, belonging to a gang … my son's crime is that he was walking down the road looking for a bus that would take him home. Our crime is living in a country where the justice system supports racist murderers against innocent people. The value that this white, racist country puts on black lives is evident. But still, we followed all the steps open to us, but one by one the doors were closed in our faces. In my opinion, what happened was the way of the judicial system making a clear statement, to make clear to black people that in this country, that before the law, their lives were worth nothing. (Greengrass, 1999, based on Lawrence, 1999, 341–2)

Baroness Lawrence spoke about how, even though she felt extremely angry on many occasions, she couldn't show it, least of all to the white media. In her acute experiences of how black people were regarded as criminals, Doreen Lawrence was arguably all too aware of the 'Angry Black Women' stereotype that Ashley posits:

> such stereotypes include the myth of the angry Black woman that characterizes these women as aggressive, ill tempered, illogical, overbearing, hostile, and ignorant without provocation. (2014: 2)

The historicity of the stereotype of the Strong Black Mother, one who endures, one who does not feel pain or show emotion, has been well documented (Dance 1979, hooks 1992, Hill Collins, 2000). Indeed, these 'emotionless' black mothers have been the subject of some black writers, as Dance explores. In these literatures the relationship between the black mother and her son is captured through the notion of the Madonna and Eve, the latter succumbing to the lure of white society, 'and that this Black Eve offers to her Black men the poisonous apple that will destroy him, that will repress his spirit and vitality, kill his pride in his Blackness, and render him impotent in a hostile white world (1979: 124).

For Dance, the antithetical Madonna figure is a woman 'who suffers the indignities of slavery; sets out on the quest for freedom; embodies the unfulfilled dreams, the suffering, the bitter struggles, the endurance, and the strength of her people; and who finally overcomes' (1979: 124). One can argue that the lived experience of contemporary black motherhood has no relation to these biblical analogies but, as Roberts points out, 'American culture reveres no Black Madonna; it upholds no popular image of a black mother nurturing her child' (1994: 874).

Lawson Bush (2004) argues that although mothering issues can be similar for white mothers raising white sons and black mothers raising black sons, the most pertinent difference is that the black mothers are forging, developing and maintaining mother-son relationships in the context of white supremacy. Of course, the white mother raising black sons also requires further exploration but the black mother, from African enslavement to contemporary society, bears a particularly heavy burden in the complex racial socialization of her black children into an often antagonistic society. The black mother must cope with the psychosocial effects of teaching her children how to operate and negotiate life while at all times being mindful of any interactions with the police in order to even stay alive within white systemic, structural and institutional racism.

Criminalization, policing and concern for black lives

Contemporary UK statistics show that the police's use of physical restraint is more prevalent on black and minority ethnic people than on whites. Proportionally more black people have died in police custody than white people, and police use greater force towards black people with mental health problems (Bulman, 2018). So it is not surprising that the black community have little confidence in those who police them.

Mark Duggan's death in 2011 and the death in 2017 of four young black men in police custody – Edson da Costa, Darren Cumberbatch, Shane Bryant and Rashan Charles – are among the fatal encounters that lead critics and activists to contend that black people receive much harsher treatment than white people in every part of the mental health and criminal justice system. Statistics also show unconscious bias and racial profiling as playing a major part in unequal treatment. Although stop and searches have fallen across all ethnic groups since 2017, they did so at different rates. Stops of white people have fallen most markedly (28 per cent), and although stops of black people have fallen by 11 per cent, they are still more than eight times more likely to be stopped than those who are white (Hargreaves, J., Husband, H. Linehan, C., 2017). The Lammy Review of the UK criminal justice system (referred to in earlier chapters) shows evidence that despite making up just 14 per cent of the population, minority ethnic men and women make up 25 per cent of prisoners, while over 40 per cent of young people in custody are from black backgrounds (Lammy, 2017: 3). An insightful study by Henning (2018) points to the fact that white police officers tend to overestimate the ages of black boys and underestimate the ages of their white peers. Moreover, Henning's work posits that black boys who experience harassment and discrimination from white police officers are left with hugely negative attitudes toward the police as they grow to adulthood.

Black British feminists facing up to such injustices

In light of the black youth crisis we have on our hands, Etienne (2016) draws attention to black feminist epistemology as being ethically bound to shared accountability and social responsibility. Strident African-American activists and intellectuals such as Angela Davis, Audre Lorde, bell hooks and Patricia Hill Collins have created a distinct theoretical standpoint of the black feminist. In the words of Hill Collins: 'Black women intellectuals have laid a vital analytic foundation for a distinctive standpoint on self, community and society and, in doing so, created a black women's intellectual tradition' (2000: 45). African-American feminists maintain that 'feminism is white' and take an oppositional standpoint in which black women are the speaking subjects. However, the paucity of black female academics in the UK who would or could describe themselves thus, means that we are between a rock and a hard place in trying to carve out a space to talk and write about race in an arena that is not dominated and silenced by African-American discourse. Siana Bangura observes:

> As with all aspects of black life, American voices are louder – from literature to music to visual art, television and the world of social media – the black American experience is conflated with the experience of every other black person in the West. The single-narrative strikes again. (Bangura, 2015: 45)

As black feminist Heidi Mirza argues: 'To be black and be British is to be unnamed in official discourse' (1997: 3), and this, she argues, has created an unforgivable blind spot in much mainstream analysis. Her point informs my concern in this chapter to develop my thinking through my personal history of racialized encounters so I can explore the possible impact of engaging with black communities on police diversity training. I set out to comprehend the challenges of race in diversity training and how we can think about what is being brought into the training space and to determine what this might mean for black youth in their engagement with police. I investigate the components of diversity training in policing and explore the unintended consequences when of race becomes the topic. I begin with examining my feelings about the historical legacy of African enslavement by Europeans.

Roots of pain and anger

In June 2018, I was in a Reading Room of the British Library, thinking about black youth, British policing and why I believed my voice as a black mother mattered. On my way out I stopped to look at the Windrush exhibition on display on the first floor (*Windrush: Songs in a Strange Land*, 2018). I was focused on the explanations of European enslavement of Africans and ensuing British colonization of African and Caribbean lands. One archived display was of an advertisement page of *The Antigua Gazette* dated 20 June 1816. I read, among the various items for sale, a consignment of limes, a gold hunting watch, and:

> Slaves, Rachel, a good Washer and her son Anthony 13 years of age; Robert a stout healthy Boy, Lewis, a ditto, 8 years of age; Lucretia, a healthy Girl, 5 years of age; The 3 latter have lost their Mother and may be sold separate. They are offered at a low price, as their owner has no use for them. For particulars please apply to the Office of Sears & Greenway.

Another advertisement displayed offered a reward to whomever could 'apprehend and deliver' Patty, a Negro woman runaway slave being 'the property of Mr A.H. Adams' (British Library, 2018). At that moment, standing in the institutionally white space of the British Library, I felt anguish and anger about the degradation of the black women and black children, of the devastating legacy of the selling off of black souls and the horrors of African chattel slavery, and its present-day ramifications for black families.

'Hard policing': Young black men fighting back

Moving on in the exhibition, I recognized my 'self' in the 1980s black anti-police protest photographs. At this point in my teenage years, from being called 'half-caste' or 'red-skinned' by others, I self-identified as black. In these photographs I recognized the fashion, the hairstyles and the need to protest. The 1970s and 80s were the years when I was part of a movement where teenagers recognized that, unlike their parents, Britain was their country of birth and they had a legal right to be here. This was a time where we 'followed' sound systems that were either soul or reggae, but whichever group one aligned oneself with, we all fell in and out of love in the 1970s, dancing to British Lovers Rock Janet Kay, Louisa Mark, and Jean Adebambo to mention a few. This was a time when a West Indian community showed the *Staying Power* examined in Peter Fryer's 1984 book of that name. However, this was also a time of severe police harassment of black communities, particularly, but not solely, of young black men. I remember seeing young black men being hassled or arrested by white police officers as they came out of a club. The dreaded police 'Bully Vans' (where black boys were often beaten up) sometimes sat outside the clubs as a real or imagined threat to us.

In April 1981, in response to a reported high level of street robbery in Brixton, the Metropolitan Police, bolstered by officers from the infamous Special Control Group, began 'Operation Swamp' based on the British 'sus' law. A retired police officer I interviewed during my research said of this period: 'That was our MO – go down to Brixton, jump out of the van and arrest or beat up as many black men as we could.' He told me about the canteen culture that prevailed: that 'if they didn't catch a black boy doing or having something illegal, they were just 'sorting them out' for doing something illegal in the past or the future. There were many reports of planting or fabricating evidence on 'suspects' during this era. The Black People's Day of Action took place on 2 March 1981 and photographs of it are included in the British Library exhibition. It was an overwhelmingly peaceful march, but *The Sun* newspaper reported the event with the headline 'The Day the Blacks Went Riot In London' (Warner, 2017). There was anger in black communities over the police and politicians' attitudes to the tragic New Cross Fire in which 13 black teenagers died, and aggressive racist Swamp 81 policing. Violent rioting took place in Brixton for three days, with documents reporting black youth' – not wider white society – as 'the enemy'.

Surveillance, black bodies, enslavement and policing

In my research on the policing of, and impact on black bodies, I have come to learn that the embryo of many contemporary American policing departments is the white slave patrols of the Antebellum South. These patrols that were formed of white men incentivized to protect the economic order and interests of white plantation owners by capturing and abusing black bodies owned during African chattel slavery. Apart from the practice of lynching, many activists have drawn parallels with US and UK policing strategies engendering 'colonial-style paramilitary methods' to police black neighbourhoods (Cashmore and McLaughlin 1991: 34). The Institute of Race Relations (IRR) documented how the Metropolitan Police in the 1980s moved from individual 'law and order' policing to 'public order' strategies when policing black communities (IRR, 1987: 2). Specially trained riot squads such as the Special Patrol Group (SPG) gained notoriety for their violent and racist tactics. A search of SPG police lockers after a National Front protest in 1979 revealed a number of unauthorized weapons, including a rhino whip, a customized lead weight truncheon and a sledge-hammer (IRR, 1987: 3).

Puwar (2004) posits that the black body occupies a particular place in relation to questions of identity, power and subjectivity, and is regarded by white supremacists as having come from somewhere savage and uncivilized that necessitates control and taming (Puwar, 2004: 21). Drawing on the archives and legacy of transatlantic slavery studies to analyse how race structures the contemporary surveillance of black bodies, Simone Browne observes that 'Surveillance is nothing new to black folks. It is the fact of anti-blackness' (2015: 10). She furthers Fanon's (1986) work on the negative psychical effects of epidermalized surveillance of black subjects in her work *Dark Matters: On the Surveillance of Blackness*. Browne avers that we can 'take transatlantic slavery as antecedent to contemporary surveillance technologies and practices, as they concern inventories of ships' cargo ... biometric identification by branding the slave's body with hot irons, slave markets and auction blocks as exercises of synoptic power where the many watched the few ...' (2015: 12).

Blaming the 'single West Indian mother'

Following the 1981 Brixton disturbances, Conservative Prime Minister Margaret Thatcher was reported in *The Times* on 10 July 1981, asking what the government could do if the parents concerned could not control the actions of their children (Solomos and Rackett, 1991: 55). *The Scarman Report* (1982) attributed the drift of African-Caribbean youth into crime and violence to weak family units, weakened through migration in which West Indian traditional family structures, especially the roles of 'single West Indian mothers' at the centre of those families, were being undermined by new demands, such as female paid work (1982). As we have seen, black people are often thus stereotyped, to provide a diversionary tactic to the 'real' issue. Scarman's 'single West Indian mother' is to blame for her lack of control of her inherently criminal offspring. What goes unremarked in the report is any critique of the invisible measure of Single Black Motherhood as against idealized White Married Motherhood. In an analysis of stereotypes of black women, Roberts argues that 'modern social pundits from Daniel Patrick Moynihan to Charles Murray have held black single mothers responsible for the disintegration of the black family and the black community's consequent despair' (1994: 874).

When I was married, I suppose on reflection that I felt 'respectable' while having four children, but when my status changed to 'single mother' I became acutely aware of the negative images of me and my children, especially as I lived in a predominantly white middle-class area. I overcompensated to ensure that my children were the most well-behaved wherever they went. In an analysis of black women stereotypes, Roberts observes that:

> The reason for society's bleak assessment is not only the belief that black mothers are likely to corrupt their children, but that black children are predisposed to corruption. Blaming single mothers for 'nurturing a next generation of pathology' stigmatizes not only mothers but their children as well. The powerful Western image of childhood innocence does not seem to benefit black children. Black children are born guilty. They are potential menaces-criminals, crackheads and welfare mothers waiting to happen. (1994: 874)

Black mothers, I argue, project both a conscious and unconscious value-coded repertoire of white-sanctioned behaviour that psychosocially regulates and controls her black child.

Engaging with racial awareness training in an inner-city UK police service

The Scarman Report made notable recommendations for police services but, particularly pertinent here, it was documented that police officer recruits should receive at least six months' training to be more prepared to police a multi-cultural society. Lord Scarman concluded that:

> the disorders were communal disturbances arising from a complex political, social and economic situation, which is not special to Brixton. There was a strong racial element in the disorders, but they were not a race riot. The riots were essentially an outburst of anger and resentment by young black people against the police. (1982: 65)

This appears commendable, on consideration of these recommendations. However, what is the reality of six months of diversity training for police work in culturally diverse urban areas where tensions exist between the police and the black community?

Years after Stephen Lawrence's murder in 1993, Recommendations 48–54 of Macpherson's *Stephen Lawrence Inquiry* (1999) were that racism awareness and valuing cultural diversity training should be undertaken by all employees in all UK police services. The Metropolitan Police Service Black Police Association (MBPA) presented the following statement to the Inquiry:

> A second source of institutional racism is our culture, our culture within the police service. Much has been said about our culture, the canteen culture, the occupational culture. How and why does that impact on individuals, black individuals on the street? Well, we would say the occupational culture within the police service, given the fact that the majority of police officers are white, tends to be the white experience, the white beliefs and values. Given the fact that these predominantly white officers only meet members of the black community in confrontational situations, they tend to stereotype black people in general. This can lead to all sorts of negative views and assumptions about black people, so we should not underestimate the occupational culture within the police service as being a primary source of institutional racism in the way that we differentially treat black people.

While on an internship with an inner-city UK police service some years ago, I had the unforgettable experience of participating in/observing several Community Race Relations (CRR) workshops. It was hugely informative but rather disappointing.

The problem of 'race' in diversity training

How was race defined, imagined and understood in CRR training? The CRR workshops were conducted in an experiential group setting, led by a facilitator and attended by staff and police officers, most of whom were white British. Stuart Hall (1994) asserts that there is a 'problem of race' for white society. I surmise that if race were not perceived as a problem, there would have been no CRR training in the first place. It is a fundamental part of my enquiry to explore what race might mean for white people in diversity training today and, therefore, how race has been historically and contextually defined, constructed and theorized. Although this chapter attempts to make some sense of contemporary issues of race and police diversity training, it is irrefutable that historical notions of race have proved contested and divisive. Arguably the dialectics of race in modern Britain have attempted to expunge historical racist ideology and practice, at least politically, by what Pitcher describes as 'revisionist narratives' (2009: 14). Pitcher furthers Hall's ideas and presents a contemporary paradox that suggests that 'dominant discourses of race have arguably resulted in a situation where anti-racist discourses sit alongside — and are to a significant extent intertwined with – continuing racist practices' (2009: 15). Anti-racist discourse requires, if not compels, us to think about race 'backwards', acknowledging the reality of difference, while reflecting on what the 'anti-' really means.

Participants undergoing diversity training need to think about the 'beginning', or what might be going on with their ideas of race. As a participant of the training (using myself as an example here), I will draw on many factors to consider the scenarios presented to me: my age, my heritage and my personal experiences of racialization. If the diversity training is experiential, the 'race' part of it will be presented to the group as an example of an anti-racist stance. For instance, a typical scenario might be as follows: 'While in a team meeting, Ahmed makes disparaging remarks about a female co-worker. It is the first time you have heard Ahmed make such a disrespectful remark. What should you do?'

As I haven't had much contact with Asian males, I would have to draw on the knowledge I do have, fill in the gaps I don't know, and do so in a way that is mindful of being judged by others in the room. I might not even recognize that the 'anti-racist' scenario itself is stereotypically racist, as it assumes that 'Ahmed' is an Asian heterosexual male and so is sexist by nature. Gordon Allport defined a stereotype as 'an exaggerated belief associated with a category', and that 'Its function is to justify (rationalize) our conduct in relation to that category' (1979: 191).

If I worked in a majority white institution, I might consider that Ahmed's co-worker in the scenario in question is white and heterosexual. If my contact with Asian males has been virtually nil, I would most likely draw on high profile media reports of, say, the Asian Rotherham paedophile ring, 9/11, Jihadist extremism, Boris Johnson's Muslim women 'letterbox' comments. While realizing these are all negative representations, I will have a psychological struggle in dealing with my thoughts in what I determine to be a politically correct environment. Although a good facilitator should then deconstruct the participants' (my) assumptions (i.e. that Ahmed is heterosexual and the co-worker is white), this requires intense emotional work by each participant and we will all undergo cognitive dissonance. Such is the 'backlash', the difficulties and antagonisms of the topic of race within diversity training that push employees through unwanted, mentally depleting exercises. Solórzano's argument is useful here. He suggests that 'when we think of welfare, crime, drugs, immigrants, and educational problems, we racialize these issues by painting stereotypic portraits of People of Color' (Solórzano 1997: 10). The stereotyping of black people, particularly males, as criminal, morally reprehensible and dangerous is ingrained in Western ahistoricism and maintained through racist institutional structures, policies and practices. All this has serious implications for the way black youth have been policed and are policed today.

Training participants who display emotional toil

When observing CRR training, I was particularly struck by the varying degrees of emotional toil and turmoil of the 'journey' for most participants, something I had not hitherto considered or experienced as part of employee training or workshops. Many participants appeared to be unsure of how 'to be' in the workshop sessions. For example, several white police staff members thought the workshop sessions were going to help explain the 'latest terminology' for describing ethnic minority groups. One staff member, who was not a police officer, asked, 'Can we say half-caste anymore?' Another asked: 'I'm uncomfortable saying "black" as I'm white. Can I say black?'

In another session a white male traffic warden inquired: 'Are Yardies religious – because if they were, they wouldn't do such horrible things?' I admit that it was difficult not to roll my eyes. I observed that a minority of people in the room felt as I did, but others were clearly uncomfortable with the question and the mood in the room changed. I was present in the post-workshop debriefing session, where the workshop trainers' consensus was that the traffic warden and his question were 'a bit weird'.

When writing up my field notes that evening, I wondered whether the traffic warden wasn't weird but, rather, brave enough or stupid enough to raise his head above the parapet to actually ask a question on a topic that some participants appeared to know nothing about. Others in the room felt just as ignorant but didn't say anything, and others did not care about knowing nothing at all about race and racism. Why did I consider the traffic warden might be brave or stupid? Why did the trainers think him weird? The 'it' was 'race', and how certain bodies were imagined and verbalized clearly created feelings and emotions on individual and group levels. It was becoming apparent to me that the compulsory workshops were far more emotionally complex and complicated in ways and at levels than I had realized. Ballard and Parveen surmise that employees taking part in such programmes 'will not only have been told in no uncertain terms that racism is not only morally intolerable but is also a serious disciplinary offence' (2008: 4). As Alhejji (2015) points out, given that the effectiveness of diversity training programmes might enhance employee engagement when implementation is associated with rewards or the avoidance of sanctions, how effective can it be for white police officers to be compulsorily trained to engage with black youth in ways other than those that are invariably hostile? Superintendent Roach, the Metropolitan Police Community Relations liaison in stated in 1978 that:

> It is not part of community relations training in the Metropolitan Police to attempt to 'convert' an officer to a particular point of view or to change personal or political opinions. The purpose is rather to inculcate an understanding of the strategic importance of good police/community relations. (IRR, 1987: 67)

There are many members of the black community today who would argue that this is still the view of many white officers some 40 years later, in that black youth are the problem, and not white policing strategies. How might these defensive feelings impact on white police officers' engagement with black youth?

Exploring race and whiteness in police diversity training

To speak of race in a contemporary context is not to deny the intersectionality of gender, class, religion and other differences; rather, it is to see how race is still often the modality through which many of these differences are experienced (Hall, 1994). In my experience of programmes since the CRR, I've seen participants who have seethed, boiled over or fumed about race. The point I want to make is that although participants are being trained or educated about race or diversity, there is little recognition in the training programmes, from conception to delivery, that the participants in the process are themselves racialized and diverse. Years of subjective experiences and a sense of identity in a cultural milieu affect a person's creation of meaning and production of knowledge, yet this is seldom acknowledged in a 'one-fits-all' training session. I contend, moreover, that one of the reasons for such turbulent and often toxic feelings is that participants bring their individual 'knowing' or 'common sense' about race into the programme, and this inevitably presents itself as problematic to the collective and the training objectives.

These observations and experiences lead me to accept that anxiety and defensiveness are always present in the room when discussing race in experiential, as opposed to unobserved e-learning, diversity training. What colours these feelings? Hollway and Jefferson aver that:

> The concept of an anxious, defended subject is simultaneously psychic and social. It is psychic because it is a product of a unique biography of anxiety-provoking life-events and the manner in which they have been unconsciously defended against. (2000: 24)

Alhejji makes the point that much diversity work 'focuses on the dynamic of minority-group oppression in majority-dominated social systems'. (2015: 15)

I argue that both an individual and an organization can be a defended subject, by invoking the emotional labour of not wanting to be regarded as racist. Psychologists Richeson and Trawalter's (2005) research suggests that many white people find 'interracial contact' mentally 'depleting', particularly in a politically correct context.

Placing anti-racism training in a policing context

Sara Ahmed's *On Being Included, Racism and Diversity in Institutional Life* (2012) argues that documents concerning diversity give institutions a physical form and these need to be tracked to see what they do. Given that institutions in the UK are predominantly white spaces, Ballard and Parveen's discussion of white middle-class professionals and their workplace attitudes to racism is useful for exploring what might recede from view:

> to the extent that 'racism' so envisaged is a product of intellectual and moral inadequacy, it follows that whilst such attitudes may be sustained by members of the lower social order, they are by definition the antithesis of the attitudes found among their educated and sophisticated social superiors. (2008: 4)

Ahmed's work on racism and diversity in institutional life gives an account of the symbolic rather than the actual commitment to diversity within institutional whiteness.

My concern is to develop an intersectional analysis of the discursive links and disjunctions within and between discourses of theory and practice of racialization within the institutionally white space of UK policing to develop better strategies for inclusivity and anti-racism, particularly with black youth. I restate, many UK police services have had a turbulent and antagonistic relationship with much of the black community for many years, most notably exposed by the enduring tragic legacy of the racially motivated killing of Stephen Lawrence in 1993, the mishandling of the case and the subsequent Macpherson Report in 1999 that found the Metropolitan Police to be 'institutionally racist'. Dalal suggests that the consequent change to the 1976 UK Race Relations (Amendment Act) 2000, which requires public bodies to provide mandatory diversity training to promote racial equality and consider the impact of policies and procedure on racial equality within the organization occurred 'because the status quo is not sufficient' (Dalal, 2012: 107).

Conclusion

The 2011 Census evidences grim statistics of the lived reality for black youth in the UK. Compared to their white British peers, black Caribbean pupils are twice as likely to be temporarily excluded and three times as likely to be permanently excluded from school. Black Caribbean people are 9.6 times more likely to be stopped and searched and 3.8 times more likely to be arrested. Furthermore, they have the highest rate of detention under the Mental Health Act 1983 (Race Disparity Unit, 2019). Lindsay (1994) argues that as many institutions are centuries old, organizational strategies and implementations were created through a Eurocentric discourse where voices of difference did not need to be considered. 'Difference' is therefore an add-on for institutions – as is evident from the dearth of black academics, teachers, judges, police officers, politicians and leaders in white institutions, and the impossibility of making any significant inroads to change those statistics when black youth are impeded in their education.

As a black woman and mother, in deep thought at the British Library, I was haunted by the thought of 'Rachel' being hunted down, and the fate of the unnamed mother of 'Robert', 'Lewis' and 'Lucretia' who, being 'lost' to them, presumably had untimely deaths. Dorothy Roberts in her article on black mothers' work writes (quoting from Toni Morrison's *Beloved*) that when enslaved family members were auctioned off to different masters, 'slave mothers knew the regular pain of seeing their loved ones "rented out, loaned out, bought up, brought back, stored up, mortgaged, won, stolen or seized"' (Roberts, 1994: 875). I thought how, centuries later, the mothers of the New Cross Fire victims, Stephen Lawrence, Edson da Costa, Darren Cumberbatch, Shane Bryant and Rashan Charles and Mark Duggan lost their loved black children to untimely deaths. Maya Angelou wisely observed:

> There is a kind of strength that is most frightening in Black women. It's as if a steel rod runs right through her head down to the feet. And I believe that we have to thank Black women not only for keeping the Black family alive, but [also] the white family … Because Black women have nursed a nation of strangers. For hundreds of years, they literally nursed babies at their breasts who they knew, when they grew up, would rape their daughters and kill their sons. (cited in Elliott, 1989)

Angela J. Davis makes a crucial point when she writes: 'a black boy's flight from the police is just as likely to be a protective measure to avoid violence as it is to result from consciousness of guilt' (2018: 86). Negative and vicarious experiences that black youth have encountered with institutionally white policing has engendered them unworthy of dignity, humanity and police protection, and this is why police training, on diversity or otherwise, needs to deal with the problems of black youth–police relations rather than, as I was told several times in my interviews, that 'race is a golden thread that runs through all training'.

In her autoethnography, 'I am an angry black woman', Rachel Griffin (2012) describes her emotionality, publicly expressing her pain at what might be perceived by hegemonic others as essentialist. However, the insistence of black women on using self-definitions to frame their work is incredibly powerful. It is core to the black feminist agenda, driving forward Lorde's idea (1992) that anger is positively productive. Research into how race is spoken about, not spoken about, experienced, taught, managed and interpellated within a predominantly white organization requires other conceptual tools that provide a synthesis of sociological, psychoanalytical, linguistic and political perspectives. As an Angry Black Woman in higher education I will continue to pick up Lorde's 'master's tools' and keep chipping away at the white block of institutional whiteness and racism.

References

Ahmed, S. (2012) *On Being Included: Racism and diversity in institutional life.* Durham, NC: Duke University Press.

Alhejji, H. (2015) 'An Analysis of the Influence of Internal and External Factors on Diversity Training Design: A case study of a multinational corporation in Saudi Arabia'. Unpublished PhD thesis, University of Limerick.

Allport, G.W. (1979) *The Nature of Prejudice.* Reading, MA: Addison-Wesley.

Ashley, W. (2014) 'The angry black woman: The impact of pejorative stereotypes on psychotherapy with black women'. *Social Work in Public Health,* 29 (1), 27–34.

Ballard, R. and Parveen, T. (2008) 'Minority professionals' experience of marginalisation and exclusion: The rules of ethnic engagement'. In Eade, J., Barrett, M., Flood, C. and Race, R. (eds) *Advancing Multi-culturalism, Post 7/7.* Newcastle upon Tyne: Cambridge Scholars Publishing, 73–96.

Bangura, S. (2015) 'I too am black and a feminist: On the importance of black British feminism'. *Media Diversified,* 13 March. Online. https://tinyurl.com/vcqds35 (accessed 11 December 2019).

BBC (2018) *Stephen: The Murder That Changed a Nation.* 3 episodes. BBC One Television, 17–19 April.

British Library (2018) *Windrush: Songs in a strange land.* Exhibition held at the British Library, London, 1 June–21 October 2018.

Browne, S. (2015) *Dark Matters: On the surveillance of blackness.* Durham, NC: Duke University Press.

Bulman, M. (2018) 'Police custody deaths hit highest level in decade after 64per cent increase in a year'. *The Independent*, 25 July. Online. https://tinyurl.com/uxkfnjb (accessed 6 December 2019).

Cashmore, E. and McLaughlin, E. (eds) (1991) *Out of Order? Policing black people*. London: Routledge.

Dalal, F. (2012) *Thought Paralysis: The virtues of discrimination*. London: Karnac Books.

Dance, D.C. (1979) 'Black Eve or Madonna? A study of the antithetical views of the mother in black American literature'. In Bell, R.P., Parker, B.J. and Guy-Sheftall, B. (eds) *Sturdy Black Bridges: Visions of black women in literature*. Garden City, NY: Anchor Press/Doubleday, 123–32.

Davis, A.J. (ed.) (2018) *Policing the Black Man: Arrest, prosecution, and imprisonment*. New York: Vintage Books.

Dodd, V. (2018) 'Stephen Lawrence murder: Police say they have run out of leads'. *The Guardian*, 11 April. Online. https://tinyurl.com/y9td2pmv (accessed 6 December 2019).

Elliot, J.M. (ed.) (1989) *Conversations with Maya Angelou*. Jackson: University Press of Mississippi.

Etienne, J. (2016) *Learning in Womanist Ways: Narratives of first-generation African Caribbean women*. London: Trentham Books.

Fanon, F. (1986) *Black Skin, White Masks*. London: Pluto Press.

Greengrass, P. (1999) *The Murder of Stephen Lawrence* [TV film]. Manchester: Granada Television.

Griffin, R.A. (2012) 'I am an angry black woman: Black feminist autoethnography, voice, and resistance'. *Women's Studies in Communication*, 35 (2), 138–57.

Hall, S. (1994) 'Cultural identity and diaspora'. In Williams, P. and Chrisman, L. (eds) *Colonial Discourse and Post-Colonial Theory: A reader*. New York: Columbia University Press, 392–403.

Hargreaves, J., Husband, H. and Linehan, C. (2017) *Police Workforce, England and Wales, 31 March 2017* (Statistical Bulletin 10/17). London: Home Office.

Henning, K. (2018) 'Boys to men: The role of policing in the socialization of black boys'. In Davis, A.J. (ed.) *Policing the Black Man: Arrest, prosecution, and imprisonment*. New York: Vintage Books, 57–94.

Hill Collins, P. (2000) *Black Feminist Thought: Knowledge, consciousness, and the politics of empowerment*. 2nd ed. New York: Routledge.

Hollway, W. and Jefferson, T. (2000) *Doing Qualitative Research Differently: Free association, narrative and interview method*. London: SAGE Publications.

hooks, b. (1992) *Black Looks: Race and representation*. New York: Routledge.

IRR (Institute of Race Relations) (1987) *Policing against Black People*. London: Institute of Race Relations.

Lammy, D. (2017) *The Lammy Review: An independent review into the treatment of, and outcomes for, black, Asian and minority ethnic individuals in the criminal justice system*. London: Lammy Review. Online. https://tinyurl.com/yyctz8zf (accessed 9 December 2019).

Lawrence, D. (1999) Address to the Stephen Lawrence Inquest. Quoted in Macpherson, W. *The Stephen Lawrence Inquiry*, 341–2. Document reference Cm 4262-I. London: UK Parliament. Online. https://assets.publishing.service. gov.uk/government/uploads/system/uploads/attachment_data/file/277111/4262. pdf (accessed 3 August 2018).

Lawson Bush, V. (2004) 'How black mothers participate in the development of manhood and masculinity: What do we know about black mothers and their sons?'. *Journal of Negro Education*, 73 (4), 381–91.

Lindsay, C. (1994) 'Things that go wrong in diversity training: Conceptualization and change with ethnic identity models'. *Journal of Organizational Change Management*, 7 (6), 18–33.

Lorde, A. (1992) 'Age, race, class, and sex: Women redefining difference'. In Andersen, M.L. and Hill Collins, P. (eds) *Race, Class, and Gender: An anthology*. Belmont, CA: Wadsworth, 495–502.

Mirza, H.S. (ed.) (1997) *Black British Feminism: A reader*. London: Routledge.

Morrison, T. (1992) *Playing in the Dark: Whiteness and the literary imagination*. Cambridge, MA: Harvard University Press.

Pitcher, B. (2009) *The Politics of Multi-culturalism: Race and racism in contemporary Britain*. Basingstoke: Palgrave Macmillan.

Puwar, N. (2004) *Space Invaders: Race, gender and bodies out of place*. Oxford: Berg.

Race Disparity Unit (2019) 'Ethnicity facts and figures: Black Caribbean ethnic group'. Online. https://tinyurl.com/seblomu (accessed 11 December 2019).

Richeson, J.A. and Trawalter, S. (2005) 'Why do interracial interactions impair executive function? A resource depletion account'. *Journal of Personality and Social Psychology*, 88 (6), 934–47.

Roberts, D.E. (1994) 'The value of black mothers' work'. *Connecticut Law Review*, 26 (3): 871–8. Online. https://tinyurl.com/sytcjj2 (accessed 30 January 2020).

Scarman, L.G. (1982) *The Scarman Report: The Brixton Disorders 10–12 April 1981: Report of an inquiry*. Harmondsworth: Penguin.

Solomos, J. and Rackett, T. (1991) 'Policing and urban unrest: Problem constitution and policy response'. In Cashmore, E. and McLaughlin, E. (eds) *Out of Order? Policing black people*. London: Routledge, 42–64.

Solórzano, D.G. (1997) 'Images and words that wound: Critical race theory, racial stereotyping, and teacher education'. *Teacher Education Quarterly*, 24 (3), 5–19.

Warner, T. (2017) '9 important London Black History landmarks: Black Peoples' Day of Action, 1981'. Online. https://tinyurl.com/wq9bp78 (accessed 11 December 2019).

Chapter 8

Educating Ryan: Black youth surviving a British education system

Jan Etienne and Dawn Joseph

Introduction

Using highlights from case study interview, this chapter reveals the experiences of a black mother and the steps she took to secure a successful academic education for her son. At the age of 50 she is about to complete her postgraduate studies in criminology and reflects on how she raised her son with support from her mother. She reflects on what she considers to be an educational success story at a troubled time on the streets, and the challenges she faced as a black single mother. As violence among black youth rises, she offers advice to other single parents on bringing up a male child in the absence of a father. She considers her son's early years' education on the Caribbean island of Dominica, which she regards as a critical start to his educational success. To what extent do transnational and kinship links influence the education of the black British child?

Letter to my son Ryan

My dear Ryan,

As we marked your 29th birthday last week (don't get depressed – you're still young!) the news continues to deliver more accounts of young black people (who look like you) being killed senselessly on London's streets. As it's the last year of your 20s, I feel compelled to reflect on how we managed to avoid you being one of those names that, sadly, is forgotten by most people who didn't have a personal connection to them.

Having grown up without my own dad in my life, I was determined that, if I had kids, it would be different for them. Life experience burst that bubble. Despite your dad and me being young and in love, the responsibilities of being a parent were too much for him. In the early 90s he was earning good money and getting a lot of female attention, which he found too good for him to settle down – and I wasn't prepared to share him. To ensure that our split would be permanent, I decided to join your Gran in the first chapter of her return to Dominica in 1993. I would love to say that it was part of my big plan – but it wasn't. And I'm not sure if you remember, but you, your gran and me had some tough times in Dominica, but we got through it.

Hindsight is a wonderful thing. If this story was to be embellished, this would have been all part of the plan but in reality, it was a series of events that seemed to work out well for us, all things considered. I believe that the fact that you started pre-school back in Dominica (at the age of 3½) gave you a really good head start when you returned to London when you were 8. Yes, we were frustrated that you seemed to go backwards then but it did mean that you were still well ahead of everyone else and, of course, you were a very clever child (you took after your Mum – smile).

Despite a few wobbles, your school years passed without incident. Your most annoying quality as a child probably followed you into manhood: being very laid back (about your school work too!). However, you excelled in your studies and were entered to do your Maths GCSE a year earlier than you were meant to. You managed to get 10 GCSEs without breaking a sweat. You stayed on at sixth form and were one of the highest performers nationally in your Business Studies A level. Four A-Levels later I wasn't very happy when you wanted to leave London and go to University in Norwich but I understood that you wanted to 'escape' from me and your gran and become your own man.

I would like to think that your teenage years were good. There were a few times where we had to pull rank and say no to you and, mostly, you took it quite well. When you were about 15 I had to accept your transition to adulthood. On one occasion you were very unhappy when I reprimanded you for being rude. On this occasion I noticed that you were seething. I remember asking you why you were so angry. I actually backed you up against the wall and asked you if you wanted to fight with me. Do you remember that? I wanted to ensure that you took any anger out on me rather than into the streets or at school. You might not have had the best of everything but you went on trips (to Canada, St Thomas Virgin Islands and Atlanta) and got what you needed. We didn't speak about your Dad much. As you became older you grew to dislike him more and more. I was worried about the impact of not having a black male role model, but this didn't faze you. I guess I had played the part of both parents. Following one of our many disagreements I remember saying that we all have roles in life and that mine (as a parent) was to make decisions about your safety; and yours (as a teenager) was to complain about it. And you being smart, I think you actually got that.

Turning to the present day. Wow, you're all grown; a university graduate and a well-rounded likeable guy, who earns more than me! We have spoken at length about what is going on in the streets at the moment. I was surprised when you told me that, in your opinion; things are not that much different than they were when you were younger. Your opinion is that the press and the fact that information spreads so quickly makes the problem seem worse than it actually is. I was interested that you felt that social media made a big difference between then and now. There are more pressures on today's teenagers. You said that there was always drugs and crime but the way it is dealt with now makes it more sinister. Listening to your reasoning, debating your political stance and your thought-provoking rationale makes me so proud to be your Mum.

Nevertheless, we are living in serious times. It doesn't take much to be affected by some of the things that are happening. I think of Kershan – he went to the same primary and secondary school as you. You had many sleepovers at his house and he spent some at ours too. What were the odds of him getting in with the wrong crowd, not doing very well at school and spending a couple stints in jail? That could have been you. I am sure that his mum wonders what went wrong. Knowing her a bit and listening to some of her single-parent struggles, there were a couple of times when I heard her say, 'Well I am done with him. He has to make up his mind for himself.' I remember thinking that I would not be done with you for some time to come!

While your grandmother and I can take some credit for the fact that we were (a little) hard on you (I don't think we did much for your 14-year-old street cred by meeting you at the school gates to ensure you came straight home), it cannot be denied that you chose your path all by yourself. You were aware of which decisions to make and, thankfully, you chose the right ones. If I never say it, please believe me when I say, I am truly grateful that the police have never knocked on my door on your account. I am grateful that I haven't needed a Visiting Order to see your face and I am grateful that you have not given me too many parental worries. I wish I could say the same for many other families. Unfortunately, this is not the case. So, knowing what we do, how can we help families to avoid going through these things?

If I had to advise a single mother (I make this choice mainly because it is the category that I fall into) of a 10-year-old son right now, there would probably be three things that I would tell her in a bid to keep him on the straight and narrow:

1. Always make your son (or children) your priority
   As we all know, things get in the way sometimes, be it work, play or adult relationships. We all like some form of escapism from our responsibilities but we have to give the children our full attention. If we don't, then someone else will. This involves sacrificing finances, time and fun – but the reward is exponential. These are some of the responsibilities that come with parenthood and they should be taken seriously. No one said it would be easy. As they get older, spend time with them to find out what motivates them. Not everyone is meant for/ or will go to university, but people have other talents such as sport, the arts or technical skills. Try to recognize, nurture and develop these skills, as they could be what might assist them in their adult years.

2. Your teenage son isn't the head of the house
   The only thing that youngsters are responsible for is their own destiny. Please avoid burdening them with any added responsibilities so that they feel like they are forced to go and find ways of making money to provide for the household. This is not the way forward. Let the children remain children for as long as they can. They should not be concerned with adult problems; they may feel forced to make bad choices and this could have dire consequences.

3. Remind the children of how important they are

    Life is hard. Yes, we know. The majority of us are struggling to make a living. We have had the children and they are our responsibility (whether their fathers are around or not). We need to ensure that they know they are wanted and loved. We need to show love to our children as much as we can. Try to protect them from family feuds and conflict. If they see this at home they will then think that it is normal on the streets. Let's try to do better for the children.

So back to you Ryan. I hope you will agree with me that these are some of the principles that you were raised on. Our journey wasn't easy but here we are. We are not at the end yet. There is much to do. I hope you can continue your journey and be a role model to your future family and our future leaders. Thank you for being the person you are. Keep striving for those goals.

Love you loads,

Mum

Jan: This letter describes a real success story?

Dawn: Yes, I don't want to sound patronizing, and I do also think that I was very lucky. Of course, I'm not the only black mother with a positive tale to tell, but for far too many of us the story is bleak. I know I must have done something right as my son is a university graduate and now earns more than me. And of course, I am very happy for him and proud of him. But no, I am not for one minute underestimating how hard other black mothers like me have to work to get things right.

Jan: In what ways might you contribute to wider debate?

Dawn: I believe what I have to say is important. I am of a certain age and I think my contribution is important. You know I genuinely want to put something back into my community by adding my voice. Right now there is so much to be done, not least tackling what can be done about these senseless killings taking place on our streets.

I am studying towards a Postgraduate Certificate in Criminology and at the same time I am doing my bit of activism by involving myself with projects aimed at tackling issues in the community, particularly around black youth.

Education, criminality and media reporting

Jan: What is your day job and in what way is it connected to your studies?

Dawn: Up until very recently, I worked for a justice reform charity. My work got me thinking about criminality. Why do we have such atrocities and why do people return to repeat offending when they appear to work it out? It's not that people are criminals. In my view it was that they didn't have education. They say black youths don't have a job and are not in education so that's why they do what they do. So if we look at those small issues then maybe we can cut reoffending rates.

Our organization helps young people prepare for court because this can be a very frightening experience.

Jan: Tell me about your views on the youth violence happening on the street.

Dawn: I'm torn about what's going on today, I think. The more of the violence the media reports, the more people become desensitized. And no, it's not right to feel like this about young lives lost through knife crimes. The media can desensitize you in a way that's bad and sometimes when I speak to my son, he says 'Mum it's not worse. It is the same as it was before. It's just that you're hearing about it now because of social media.' He seems to think it was almost as bad in his day but there was no social media to spread the news as quickly.

Parenting concerns

Dawn: But I do think young black boys are getting a bad rap. When I look at the age of some of the kids caught up in all of this I think, and I'd be hated for saying this, but I do think at times it's us, the parents, who are to blame. Honestly, sometimes (though of course not in all cases) single black mothers I know are telling their boys, in the absence of fathers, telling a child of seven: 'You are the man of the house now'. But when that kid gets to 14 and has been hearing that since the age of 7, you can't tell him he's not the man of the house anymore. So what does he do? He rebels. And I see how the child gets the blame. But I don't always think it's the fault of the child. I think it's a combination. I think it's the style of parenting.

Early years education

Jan: You said that your son started school in Dominica. How did that come about?

Dawn: We went to Dominica when he was three and came back when he was eight. As a result, he was always top of his class in the UK.

Jan: So you think that early years' education abroad was a factor in his success?

Dawn: I definitely think the Caribbean way is better and it's different. I remember being at work in Dominica one day and seeing him walking down the road. He was four years old and carrying a backpack on his back in the hot sun. His bag was full of books for his homework. When I was talking to my friends in the UK and their kids were 4, they didn't have homework but he did. I definitely think it helped that he learned to read very early.

Activism and inclusion

Jan: On the question of your activism and involvement in projects, how are you lending your voice?

Dawn: I attend meetings where we as black women are all incensed about rising knife crime among black youth but just talk. We've got to do something more. I think we have to collaborate or reach out to other organizations because they're the way in, but I know there is conflict sometimes. Even in my own organization on our board of trustees, they're all white. Yes, in London, in this day and age! I also think we have to use the people who are willing to help us. So instead of them being our enemies, we need to bring them in to organize with us. I often say: 'We can sit in this room together and get angry and black boys are still going to get killed. We need to reach out.'

Let's reach out beyond our black women's groups.

Jan: And does that include involving black men?

Dawn: We have to get black men involved. It can't be just women. Sometimes we overlook what these boys are missing by not having men in their lives.

Teacher support

Jan: How important is the role of the teacher?

Dawn: Very important. They have to teach of course, but I've seen the way some teachers stand at the school gates and bark at these children, 'Where are your shoes? Where is your shirt?' If teachers want kids to do something they have to find better ways of communicating with them. Do things differently.

You don't know what kind of morning they have had. You don't know if they ate last night. You don't know if they've slept. You have to find another way to meet them in the middle. I know it is not easy, but sometimes we overlook what kind of homes children come from.

Stop and search

Jan: What of the involvement of the police?

Dawn: Thankfully I haven't had much interaction with the police in my own life. I feel it's really difficult – you know, you see young black boys lined up against the wall being stopped and searched and you worry. Don't get me wrong – it needs to be done, but it needs to be done sensitively and correctly. This is what everyone is saying but nobody's breaking down what 'sensitively' or 'correctly' actually mean. I think in some ways the police are damned if they do and damned if they don't. Resources are limited and, just like in any other organization, there are racist police officers. I went to a talk the other day and I became aware that there are a lot of issues that we don't hear about – such as *why* there are still so many black deaths in police custody. Nobody talks about this. Nobody knows why, but you don't hear these issues discussed on social media – the media is selective. What could be going on?

Black male role models: I found myself (in the images) – I was comfortable

Dawn: I am a very optimistic person and want to be part of change making. I think we need older people involved in working with young people. We need older people who look like these young people to talk to them and tell them this is not the way. When I was doing my undergraduate study I had to interview a member of the black community who was working with young black boys. In his interview he said: 'I went to a wedding a couple of weeks ago. When we got the photographs back, the first person I looked for was myself. As soon as I found ME, I was comfortable that I could then look at everybody else.'

Jan: And what you're saying is that black boys are looking for themselves?

Dawn: Yes, that's exactly what I am saying. There are not enough positive images of black men in the media that could encourage black boys to say, 'Well I'm not going to do this, I'm going to do that instead'. There isn't enough support to help boys to make decisions like, 'No. I am not going to sell weed.' Despite the attraction of having money to buy the latest trainers, they need to have positive black (sometimes) male role models advising, 'If you go and study you might have this great job at the end of it. Without that you are probably more likely to have the police knocking on your door.' We definitely need black men in the picture.

They think if they go outside a postcode they're going to get stabbed. How do you get over that? We have to show them that postcodes don't belong to people.

Black youth, fascination with crime, discipline

Dawn: But what was so mind-blowing for me was the reaction from black youth to a recent visit to the UK by the governor of Rikers Island. The governor came here to visit a Young Offenders Institute and I accompanied him to speak to a group of young people.

Jan: And this was part of your work?

Dawn: Yes. We got a group of young people together to speak to him. They soon got into a very lively conversation. And do you know how many and what type of questions these young people asked him? I think he was overwhelmed. The young people were so interested and fascinated with what he had to say. It took me by surprise. They clearly knew a great deal about the prison already but their questions were endless. These were a few: '*What is it like? How bad is it over there? Is it degrading? How many hours are they locked up for?*' It was like they were collecting data. Yes, this is the kind of stuff that fascinates the youth of today. What does that tell us? I don't really know.

With the violence going on, I think it's what these kids are smoking. It alters their minds. What gives you the right to think you can just go and 'shank' somebody with a six-inch knife? Well. You can't be thinking straight can you?

If I see a group of black boys up to no good, I go up to them and say, 'Hey what you think you're doing?' I think I can do that. Maybe I'm being naïve but a part of me thinks I have that right because they will respect me because I look like their mum. But I could be totally wrong. But I would definitely call them out and say: 'What are you doing on this bus?'

Jan: Do you think other black mothers think the same way in this regard?

Dawn: I think a lot do. We'll just wade in there and probably think about the consequences after. I've heard a lot of people say that. A lot of them think like me. I think sometimes if you're a single parent sometimes and you're the only parent you just want to be favoured so much that you let kids get away with stuff.

Jan: Let's move on to discipline and punishment in black families.

Dawn: I think I'd say that my mum probably beat me twice in my childhood. That was discipline and punishment together. I was petrified of her. Otherwise it was just a look – she didn't have to say anything. Having said that, it probably didn't bode well for our relationship. In my 20s I still felt the animosity between us because I was always scared of her. And even up to yesterday I was telling my friend about still being worried about what my mum would say. She replied, 'Even now when you are 49 years old?' Yes – that's how it is sometimes. But my mum is quite emotional towards my son.

I remember my mum saying that when I was little (around age 4), she was going through some hard times and she considered sending me to Dominica. It was difficult for a single mother in the 70s. My mum said that when it came to it she couldn't do it. I think that would've been really interesting and wonder what type of life I would have had. But she said she just couldn't send me back.

Jan: Finally, what role would you say higher education has played in developing your thinking?

Dawn: I've always thought in a particular way but I think returning to higher education provides affirmation of my thoughts – it's the evidence. I've always thought that some people aren't treated fairly but saying 'It's not fair' isn't enough. Being in higher education has helped me get to the root of it all. It has provided some answers as to how things have got this way (Bhambra *et al.*, 2018). It gives me an insight into what can possibly be done to change things about inequality generally. I think being in education has helped me get to the root cause of things. It has opened my mind and helped me to navigate through my thinking (Narayan, 2019). That is the role that higher education has played in my life.

Conclusion: Avoiding distraction and surviving the British education system

Gunter (2017: 20) points out that in hostile, challenging environments like ours, 'race does matter'. It certainly matters to the police and the other statutory and justice sector agencies and to the professionals who disproportionately monitor, target, prosecute and convict black boys and young men. But the discussions acknowledge that tackling matters of racism in British schools also depends on black parents and their ability to navigate the system successfully and work alongside teachers. However, as Bhopal (2018) points out, this is a difficult task, as there is a great deal of evidence to suggest that challenging racism is a problem and that [white] teachers are not entirely able to understand what black children experience in the classroom. But for the black mother who has access to a particular type of bonding social capital, and kinship support, there are ways to navigate the worst forms of structural racism (as alluded to in Chapter 3) in the British education system. Opportunities for black mothers to develop additional cultural capital, particularly in securing alternative educational options for their children when they're very young, can help them to have successful educational journeys that will avoid the potential conflicts ahead. A deep interest in the safety of black children and, in particular, their interactions with and connections to the wider community were important factors in the success of this story. The narratives in this chapter point to regular, reflective, intellectual conversations between parents and children throughout their schooling. The introduction of alternative educational spaces that begin very early on can prove a strong impetus for success.

Tracey Reynolds (2004) looks at the ways in which second and third-generation young people of Caribbean descent in Britain engage in the processes of constructing ethnic identity, and the ways in which they utilize family and kinship networks and relationships. I argue that this has been influential in expanding agency for black mothers to raise their sons to follow the 'right path'. And daughters who raise their children in collaboration with their own mothers and those who are able (and have the means) to incorporate influential visits to the Caribbean, appear to do well but, as suggested in this chapter, serial migration (Phoenix and Seu, 2013) poses its own challenges for mother/daughter relationships. Reynolds (2004) argues that black mothers understand bonding social capital within a transnational context that is not exclusively confined to their local area or nation state. Strong links with the Caribbean can prove invaluable in strengthening their commitment to education. Linking social capital also allows individuals to access and link social resources transnationally, positioning their family activities within a transnational context. Dipping into education in the Caribbean can prove very effective for African Caribbean families and there are visible benefits of matriarchal family structures that can help to keep the focus on effective learning.

The Caribbean discipline, the kinship, the strong acceptance and respect for 'the motherland' are all beneficial. Some would argue that such practices help to keep black children out of harm's way and develop their focus on a successful future. Strong matriarchal links (Etienne, 2016), and the guidance of grandmothers in particular, are crucial in supporting mothers in raising and nurturing young children in single parent households.

This chapter shows how 'Educating Ryan' along a particular educational pathway led to success in higher education and employment for both mother and son. In times of increasing school exclusions among sections of the black population, could this tried-and-tested model be emulated in contemporary black British life?

References

Bhambra, G.K., Gebrial, D. and Nişancıoğlu, K. (eds) (2018) *Decolonising the University*. London: Pluto Press.

Bhopal, K. (2018) *White Privilege: The myth of a post-racial society*. Bristol: Policy Press.

Etienne, J. (2016) *Learning in Womanist Ways: Narratives of first-generation African Caribbean women*. London: Trentham Books.

Gunter, A. (2017) *Race, Gangs and Youth Violence: Policy, prevention and policing*. Bristol: Policy Press.

Narayan, Y. (2019) 'On decolonising our departments and disciplines, respectability and belonging'. *Discover Society*, 3 July. Online. https://tinyurl.com/yxk4ylzp (accessed 9 December 2019).

Phoenix, A. and Seu, B. (2013) 'Negotiating daughterhood and strangerhood: Retrospective accounts of serial migration'. *Feminism and Psychology*, 23 (3), 299–316.

Reynolds, T. (2004) 'Caribbean families, social capital and young people's diasporic identities'. London: Families and Social Capital ESRC Research Group, London South Bank University. Online. https://tinyurl.com/v5ymzyw (accessed 30 January 2020).

Part Three

Black women in higher
education, supporting and
collaborating internationally
for change

Chapter 9

And they didn't die: Black women and the silencing of activist voices

Nombuso Mathibela

Introduction

South African essayist and novelist, Lauretta Ngcobo, wrote a beautiful, haunting account of the particularity of apartheid experiences and their effects on rural Black women who struggled to survive and maintain dignity under increasingly oppressive conditions that disrupted their material, symbolic and spiritual relationship to land. In her novel, *And They Didn't Die* (1990), Ngcobo addresses the experiences of rural women in the province of Kwa-Zulu Natal who struggled to maintain a cultural and moral order largely destroyed by the imposed settler-colonial domination. Her novel is a significant contribution to Black women's anti-apartheid and anticolonial resistance in South Africa.

Despite the structured discriminations of apartheid, the experiences of Black women in urban areas in the UK show similar feelings of alienation from dominant authorities and have generated visible alternative communities at grassroots levels. Their voices are largely suppressed in conversations about strategies for tackling crucial issues such as black youth violence. Like their South African sisters, they often feel their activism has generally been obscured rather than made clearly visible in male-dominated literary communities, policy development and liberation history.

This chapter highlights the struggles and achievements of Black women in South Africa, who have contributed to a rebalancing of the liberation narrative. It offers a case study that illustrates parallels with the experiences of Black women across the African diaspora and internationally, from which important lessons can be learnt. It emphasizes the tensions within what is recorded solely as the history of racial oppression. Through focusing on South Africa's student movement, I suggest that Black women's political representation and insistence on political subjectivity and agency have surfaced partly from a collective desire to recognize the contribution of those rendered invisible and 'disappeared' from popular history. While South Africa's history, together with the brutalities experienced in popular struggles, is being publicly revealed over time, this is less the case for the internal struggles within celebrated popular movements. To offer insights into the South African narrative, I therefore examine some detailed contexts, and reflect on the lessons drawn from nationalist movements and struggles in other parts of the African continent, and the Black Consciousness Movement (BCM). Subsequently, I suggest that the resolution of some of the biggest questions plaguing present feminist political spaces, such as women's invisibility, can be delivered by a mass movement actively engaged in political struggle.

The chapter distinguishes Black women and Black non-binary people, encompassing gender identities and expressions that do not fall within cisgender, heteronormative frameworks and political concerns. The intention is not to disregard the huge differences and internal contradictions that exist between different groups of Black women but instead to acknowledge their existence and roots, embracing bell hooks's (1991) articulation of imperialist, white supremacist, capitalist patriarchy.

Archiving the present-past and silenced narratives

Much of what follows draws on insights from history and a wider regional geography of political movements that illuminate recent student movements. In 2017, Nwabisa Plaatjie, a South African theatre playwright and director involved in the Rhodes Must Fall movement at the University of Cape Town, wrote and directed a play entitled *23 years, A Month And 7 days*. The play follows the life of a young Black woman who finds herself in the university at the height of the student protests and has to contend with being caught between two worlds of great expectations. On the one hand, she carries the weight of her family's hopes of escaping poverty. On the other are students who have engaged in a political programme for free education, aiming to end exploitative labour-broking and achieve the decolonization of the university and broader society. Plaatjie produces this play amid another wave of student protest in South Africa, pushing us to examine the complexity of movement building in contemporary South Africa, which is often lost in chauvinist politics. This complexity lies at the core of this chapter's concerns.

The complexities and tensions that Plaatjie highlights compelled many of us who were enmeshed in this storm to reflect more studiously on the stories that we were complicit in silencing. These reflections also made us consider the weight of these narratives, seldom heard in the dominant discourse and popular culture of resistance within student movements. Both Plaatjie's and Ngcobo's work provide abstractions of the historical and social reality for rural or urban, young, poor, women, who often lack the necessary social capital and language that is valued in popular struggle narratives. However, such accounts, spanning three decades, also show that across spatial and temporal boundaries, Black women have been defying patriarchal histories that relegate and objectify them, imposing normative frameworks, and rendering them invisible as political agents who have, over history, contested power in national liberation movements and anticolonial struggles.

The radicalizing effects of collective alienation

My own participation was shaped by my outsider provincial status. I had lived outside Cape Town for most of my life. As a student at the University of Cape Town, generally regarded as one of the whitest and most hypermasculine universities on the African continent, I shared with other Black students a strong sense of systemic alienation (Mathibela: 2017). Like Cedric Robinson, 'my happiest and most stunning opportunities for raising hell with corruption and deceit has been with other Black people' (Kelley, 2017). In particular, it has been the struggles of Black women that have most anchored my political commitments against racial capitalism and the imposition of gendered power structures. When the Rhodes Must Fall protest began in 2015, I was beginning my final year of law school, and like many Black students, the movement became a radicalizing moment that chartered the trajectory of my political life and intellectual commitments (Matandela, 2015) against racial capitalism. I was aware of the influence of Rhodes Must Fall on UK student activist movements but less aware of the various prior educational struggles initiated by black women (Watt and Jones, 2015; Mirza, 2009; Bryan *et al.*, 1985) in earlier times in cities such as Manchester and London. The achievements of such international movements have been precipitated by conditions of collective alienation in their varying epistemic forms, among which my experiences form part of this grand narrative of disconnection and dissent.

Black women as activists and creators of struggle and ideology

It's useful to look at some historical cases elsewhere before returning to the South African context so we can better understand the complexities and tensions that underlay the later student movement. African nationalist and grassroots political organizer Hannah Kudjoe played a formidable role in Ghana's nationalist struggle for independence in 1957, and was firmly at the helm of Kwame Nkrumah's consolidation of the new nation state under the Convention's People Party (CPP) (Allman, 2009). Yet in the retellings of Ghana's independence history we rarely hear of Kudjoe and the contributions of the broader women's movement. In 1960 the All-African Women's league became Ghana's Women's league, with Kudjoe as its founder and distinctive ideologue. Despite the crucial political role that she played, the unnaming of Kudjoe became a notable feature in the dominant narrative as the struggle for independence transformed into a struggle to consolidate the new-nation state (Allman, 2009: 14). Kudjoe's fight began to slip from national public memory and her disappearance from the historical archive seems to correlate directly with the appearance of the state's hegemonic imperative (Allman, 2009: 24). The trajectory of Kudjoe's high public profile gradually diminished with the constitution of the postcolonial state and culminated in Nkrumah's insistence that the country's two largest women's groups – one being the Ghana Women's League, led by Kudjoe – should be subsumed into a single organization: the National Association of Ghana Women. This stripped Kudjoe of her autonomy and her leadership of a women's organization whose central control lay with the CPP's executive, which instilled a new culture that totally disarmed the possibilities that might have arisen from autonomous feminist organizations engaged in nationalist struggles.

In the case of Tanganyika, now Tanzania, the Tanganyika African National Union (TANU) played a significant role in the struggle for independence in East Africa. The most prominent woman nationalist leader of the TANU Women's Section, Bibi Titi Mohamed, ushered Tanzania into independence in 1961, alongside Julius Nyerere and other nationalist leaders. However, Bibi Titi was soon obscured in a liberation history that she had forged so tirelessly with other formidable women nationalists. Within three months in 1955, thousands of women from Dar es Salaam had joined the newly established nationalist party, and by the end of the year more women than men were card-carrying TANU members (Geiger, 1997: 1).

Susan Geiger suggests that Bibi Titi Mohamed and Julius Nyerere were probably the only TANU leaders whose names were well known throughout the country at independence (Geiger, 1997: 9). Yet despite her prominence, like Hannah Kudjoe in Ghana, Bibi Titi Mohamed, receives only passing mention in most accounts of Tanzanian nationalism and independence, and the thousands of female TANU activists who recognized her leadership received even less (Geiger, 1997: 9). Through Bibi Titi's story, it is possible to witness the extent to which ordinary women crafted and performed Tanganyikan nationalism's political culture despite the limitations on women's political participation and the continuing gender constraints facing Tanganyikan women (Geiger, 1997: 19). Essentially, the cultural work of the nationalist struggle was resolutely determined by Bibi Titi and her sisters. Their focus was on the unification of women under the anticolonial, nationalist struggle, and the task of undermining cultural and linguistic markers of difference that had so gravely defined relations under colonial rule (Geiger, 1997: 13).

Turning to South Africa, my focus is on the political participation of women aligned with the African National Congress (ANC), in particular, the African National Congress Women's League (ANCWL), and also the non-aligned women's organizations, the Federation of South African Women (FSAW). Many in FSAW argued that 'any women's organization that stands outside this [national liberation] struggle must stand apart from the mass of women. The [intended] hegemony of the national struggle in the construction of oppositional politics was clear' (Walker, 1991: xvii). Reservations about FSAW's ability to mobilize as an autonomous women's organization against the tide of the nationalist struggle continued to cloud the organization's trajectory. This was compounded by concerns that such a formation might compete with the ANCWL (Walker, 1991: xvii). For the ANCWL, the demands of the national liberation struggle continued to take precedence in the organization's aims, strategies and tactics, and therefore represented the largest influential bloc of members within FSAW's federation structure. FSAW gradually modelled itself along the lines of the national struggle, guided symbolically by the direction of the African National Congress, the political home of many ideologues within ANCWL and FSAW. Consequently, the focus narrowed.

The Black Consciousness Movement and the gender question

The South African Student Organization 'SASO' identified with the Black Consciousness Movement (BCM) and in 1968 it adopted the BC philosophy as a political praxis and articulation of the conditions of black people under apartheid's doctrine of white supremacy (Gqola, 2001: 131). Largely influenced by the Négritude movement of the 1930–40s, scholars such as Césaire and Senghor, black power movements in the diaspora, and the Azanian people's movements in South Africa, BC came to be defined by Steve Biko and his colleagues as follows:

> Black Consciousness is, in essence, the realization by the black man of the need to rally together with his brothers around the cause of their oppression – the blackness of their skin – and to operate as a group in order to rid themselves of the shackles that bind them to perpetual servitude. It seeks to demonstrate the lie that black is an aberration from the 'normal' which is white. It is a manifestation of a new realization that by seeking to run away from themselves and to emulate the white man, blacks are insulting the intelligence of whoever created them black. (Steve Bantu Biko, 1971)

Women's participation in BCM has been a key debate in activist scholarship, and a significant proportion of BCM women activists understood race as the central contradiction from which other forms of oppression reproduced themselves. The focus on racism as the central dividing issue meant that women were involved in BCM because they were black, not because they were women (Rampele, 1990). Moreover, the nature of their participation tended to take on a nurturing, maternal or supportive role so that women were relegated to subordinate positions and given secretarial, treasurer and fundraising duties (Rampele, 1990). Within the university, certain women began to contest male dominated space, becoming increasingly assertive and often having to act out a masculine role to maintain political power in both private and public spaces (Rampele, 1990). These experiences, which reflect earlier struggles by black women internationally (Davis, 1981), were re-articulated in the recent student movement, where many of us felt the need to take on hypermasculine expressions in order to maintain a voice. Like the experiences of some SASO women, women in the student movement often took up invisible domestic labour roles that reinforced gendered differentiation of 'work, including duties such as cleaning and catering; and such tendencies were often not systematically challenged by either women or men in leadership' (Rampele, 1990: 6).

Moreover, the sexual violence that took place within the movement was not brought to account. Rampele (1990), Gqola (2001) and others argued that the BCM's articulation of its philosophy defined exclusively Black malehood as its subject of political concern, effectively subjecting women to invisibility, abuse and the depoliticization of their experiences. BCM's linguistic structure and use of 'Man – Black Man you are on your own' is understood as illustrating the movement's blind spot to sexist language and gender inequality, thus reinforcing existing power structures (Gqola, 2001: 7).

Reflecting on SASO, scholar and activist Oshadi Magena argued that it recognized that women and men could operate equally and by extension its articulation of Black Consciousness tacitly endorsed the problematic nature of 'gender' (Mangena, 2008: 254). Mangena concedes that gender was not an organizing principle of the movement but argues that 'gender concerns were endorsed although without active intention' (Mangena, 2008: 254). Moreover, she argues that the linguistic choice of 'man', although insensitive to sexist language, denoted 'person' or in Mangena's framing 'female and male'. In line with many arguments put forward by African linguistic scholars, Mangena develops this further, explaining that 'in Bantu languages spoken in South Africa, the term for human being is 'motho' or 'umuntu', which refer directly to either a female or a male, so she argued that within BCM the term 'man' was used without any experiential or conceptual gender connotations whatever (Mangena, 2008).

The history and formation of BCM offers important lessons for the question of gender in students' movements today. The different experiences and articulations of BCM show us that a movement's philosophy and practices are totally interwoven and do not operate independently. The negation of an inclusive language and symbolic order within a movement's internal structure affects its ethos and, in this case, how women experience the movement in practice. By observing the tensions within BC over gender, my intention is not to negate its political value for Black women. In fact, the relevance of the ideas articulated by Steve Biko (1978) and others can hardly be questioned since they live on in song, protest art and the political ethos and practices of student movements across the country (Mathibela and Dlakavu, 2016), and internationally across the black diaspora. BC influences were evident in the physical spaces of universities, from the renaming of the Bremner administrative building in the University of Cape Town as Azania House and Senate House at Witswaterstrand University as Solomon Mahlangu House (Mathibela and Dlakavu, 2016). 'Graffiti signs with slogans such as "Biko Lives" appeared on Witswaterstrand University walls, while at the University of the Free State walls were spray-painted with names such as Biko House, Lillian Ngoyi House and Sobukwe School of Law' (Mathibela and Dlakavu: 2016), confirming the symbolic power of language. Moreover, founding statements of student movements like Rhodes Must Fall cite the importance of BC (Rhodes Must Fall, 2015). My critique of BC, therefore, lies chiefly in the gaps between the movement's philosophy and its practices: in the ways in which power has been asserted and consolidated, and the failures to assess internal and external gendered oppressions.

The political processes of disappearing black women

The historical struggles of black people across the globe have demonstrated different manifestations, strategies and tactics in addressing the collective problem of imperialist, white supremacist patriarchy. Yet their records conspicuously share a similar epistemic crisis of the disappearance of black women and non-binary people from archival histories. Be it the active political labour of black women in the Black Panther and Black Power movements in Britain, the political articulations of black women in grassroots movements in the USA, or the nationalist histories in Africa, their absence is conspicuous.

The tensions arising from BCM, the difficult political choices that confronted FSAW and ANCWL, and the disappearances of women's remarkable contributions from the historical record made me consider what the consolidation of power means for black women's histories. When demands pursued against the university and the state are partially or wholly realized, how will victory be memorized and by whom? In the new nation states, numerous women who had played important roles in national liberation movements found themselves marginalized politically by the new, dominant regimes, outcast into roles that ensured that they could neither threaten nor disrupt the postcolonial 'boys' club'. Susan Geiger writes, 'women's political action and history are "disappeared" in a cumulative process whereby successive written accounts reinforce and echo the silences of previous ones' (Geiger, 1997). This is not an inevitable manifestation of a patriarchal society but a constructed product of cultural, symbolic and political struggle.

The work of feminist organizers and intellectuals has challenged us to understand that in the unfolding of historical processes of decolonization and shifts towards democratization, black women have consistently asserted a political praxis that stems from a cogent analysis of political, economic and social conditions, wherever they are in the world. Therefore, any accounts that deny nuanced understanding of resistance histories will fail to address the ways in which systems of oppression dominate their subjects (Hill Collins, 1990). Such accounts also fail to recognize the complex and contested nature of liberation paradigms and processes.

The continuities of nationalist cultural tropes within the student movement

Numerous accounts, both in scholarship and in popular history, have portrayed nationalism as a necessarily hypermasculine, historical process aimed at taking power by removing the colonial rulers, and thus transforming colonial subjects into national citizens. This process is largely understood as led and made possible by a Western-educated African male elite (Geiger, 1997), but this is a linear and somewhat uncomplicated picture. However, the Tanganyikan example reveals a different trajectory of nationalism that was firmly rooted in the cultural production of the TANU Women's section. This is not a case of romanticizing: Tanganynikan women nationalists were not simply recipients or bearers of nationalism but were agents of progress and were among its major creators (Geiger, 1997).

Contemporary student activists agitating for decolonization have similarly focused on cultural production for its unifying effects by using old and new resistance songs, writings, performance pieces, and artistic installations to protest. Notably, black women were among the most progressive creators of the aesthetic, cultural and symbolic politics of this movement. They were also among the key contributors to a new political consciousness that emerged from the post-apartheid era.

The transition to democracy in South Africa after the nationalist climb-down placed gender equality concerns at the heart of democratic debates (Hassim, 2006). The democratic transition offered new possibilities for the women's movement to contest power at the national political level, thus destabilizing nationalist formulations of women's political roles (Hassim, 2006). This created the space for demands to be pursued on democratic grounds rather than through national liberation (Hassim, 2006: 129). Despite internal contradictions and ideological weaknesses, the trajectory of the women's movement showed clearly that it was organizations rooted in, and concerned with, taking up community-based issues that attracted black women into politics. New feminist politics, voices and spaces emerged from the collective labour of the national liberation movement, the promises of democratic transition and shift towards citizenship as the basis of the struggle for rights. And they evolved in ways that precipitated the conditions for some of us to make the demands that we believed to be humane. This was despite the intergenerational tensions that defined our relationships with the older activist generation, arising from irresolvable views about the past conflicting with our expectations of the future.

Articulation of theory as borne out of struggle aptly describes the rise of a persistent feminist praxis within the student movement that emerged from the systematic disappearance from historical archives of black women's political subjectivity. Black women began to mark their presence in this historical moment. Some resisted by writing, creating installations that embodied protest, and plays that revealed the complexities of movement building, such as Plaatjie's, *23 Years 7 Days And A Month*. Many performed the invisible and emotional labour that Rampele recounts of BCM earlier, by organizing food, fundraising legal fees for students arrested at the height of state repression, and ensuring securitization.

In 2016, black women at Rhodes University (later subversively renamed to 'University Currently Known As Rhodes') organized a raging protest called *#RUReferencelist* against a systemic rape culture on campus that had gone unchallenged in universities and broader society (*Daily Vox*, 2017). It began by naming 11 men students on social media as being sexual offenders, which roused students into collective action (Seddon, 2016). Intent on rounding up the listed students, the crowd gathered under *#RUReferencelist* and entered one man's residence but the university responded by calling for a police presence. It later suspended some students and imposed on others a lifetime ban from the university (Fleischack *et al.*, 2017).

At the University of Cape Town, the UCT Trans Collective staged a protest on 9 March 2016 that would alter the student movement's political terrain and its vested interest in heteronormativity, in both theory and practice (Bubblegum Club, 2016). On 5 April 2016, black women with a sjambok [whip] in one hand staged a naked protest at the University of Witwatersrand, challenging male activists who had decided to exclude black women, queers and trans people from the movement's political programme. Throughout South African universities, black women and black non-binary people stood on picket lines, marched, faced arrest and brutal treatment from the state's machinery (Ndaba, 2016), to challenge the normative cultural assumptions about political movements.

The struggle for a new consciousness: Challenges and contradictions

The student movement evolved from the unfinished process of decolonization and a quest for humanity that underpinned the ongoing historical struggle of political resistance against the colonial institutions and power formations of settler rule. This historical process of resistance, abandoned under South Africa's negotiated settlement in 1994, was resuscitated to form the basis for later struggles. As Ramose (2001) observes, there was a shared sense that South Africa had gone through a period of democratization without decolonizing, apparent in slogans like '1994 changed Fokol' that was used by Black movements predating the 2015 student movement. Some agreed with Ramose's analysis that *including* the historically oppressed in the new South Africa without addressing their claims to sovereignty represented a denial of historical justice. Indigenous sovereignty in particular was understood as a necessity because of earlier political non-recognition (Ramose, 2001) and this underpinned the political projects of many student activists who believed that this was the most just way of addressing claims to space. Others believed that 'the question of freedom in South Africa was reduced to the problem of the constitutional recognition of the 'civil rights' of the conquered peoples of South Africa' (Ramose, 2007: 320) but acknowledged that different pathways were needed to establish justice based on historical rights.

Pursuing a politic that centred on the return of stolen land and reinstating indigenous sovereignty reproduced split views. It became unclear whether indigenous sovereignty could become a mark of progress in decolonization and advance an anticolonial or postcolonial future, while avoiding the associated violence that has arisen in various manifestations of sovereignty (Motha, 2009). Much of the debate challenged the parameters of 'indigeneity', how this concept could include the diversity of oppressed people, and whether this solution could address the class formations and relations that had formed under colonial domination. Against this backdrop of contested space, varied and vibrant discussion about our political future ran through the broad-based student movement but sometimes deteriorated into corrosive divisions.

Nonetheless, in 2015 university students, workers and allied academic staff decided collectively that the political programme should start where we were. We called for colonial symbolisms and signifiers of imperial domination to be devalued. Across South Africa, students subversively renamed buildings, invoking significant black historical figures, among them Mam' Winnie Madikizela Mandela, Solomon Mahlangu and Steve Bantu Biko (Mathibela and Dlakavu, 2016). We foregrounded a longstanding demand for the decolonization of knowledge and associated assumptions so as to enable us to address questions confronting our times. We also mounted a critique against the unjustifiable paucity of black professors and demanded the employment of black lecturers, particularly black women, in higher education institutions (Rhodes Must Fall, 2015). To guide us, we drew on black archives across the global south, and especially prioritized women who had vigorously petitioned for the acquisition of knowledge and space within institutions of higher learning (Davis, 1981).

Perhaps the most striking alliance was that between the student movement and outsourced workers in the university. This became a highly effective student-worker coalition and led to a shift in labour brokering practices that had previously exploited workers through low wages, absent employment benefits, and harsh and inhumane working conditions. Not all universities achieved this victory: many workers remain outside the university system, and many others have faced universities that try to stop improved labour conditions (Adriaanse, 2017). Sadly, little has changed and, for the majority of workers, the struggle for economic and racial justice continues.

Overall, the call for decolonization emerged from the material and existential dilemma of how to resolve the question of the West in the South, not least its universalizing, neo-liberal ambitions. In Freirean terms, the student-worker dialogues began to illuminate the realities of oppression, not as a closed world with no exit but as a restrictive situation that we could transform. The demands for free, decolonized education and an end to outsourcing presented an opportunity for us to reimagine the joint roles of labour and education, while contesting the purportedly emancipatory project of post-apartheid South Africa's rainbow nation (Kamanzi, 2016) – one that had yet to be realized (Ramose, 2007: 321).

However, the struggle for new consciousness came with serious internal contradictions. What made black women a powerful and legitimizing force for mobilizing both institutionally and nationally also made some of us unpopular in wider political arenas. Threats to heteronormative sensibilities, for example challenging views that people fall into precise, complementary and 'natural' genders, caused black and queer feminist groups to be seen as antagonistic to the quest for black unity within the university. The internal contradictions and manifestations of disunity in the student movement were frequently visible in tensions between male and feminist leaders, and often inflamed by particular violent masculinities. Looking back, it seems that some of this dysfunction was a logical outcome of poor politics gone deeply wrong in the face of internal and external complexities, exacerbated by mounting militarism, and state and institutional securitization.

Intersectionality was adopted in RhodeMustFall's founding statement (Rhodes Must Fall, 2015) as a conceptual tool through which to recognize nuances of power and their effects on different groups of Black students. However, we often found ourselves so profoundly fixated with an individual subject's positionality that questions who could speak, and the individual's proximity to structural and institutional violence dominated so greatly that we became locked into the very identities that marked our collective oppression. A form of identity politics emerged, creating a political righteousness framing articulations of injustice in ways that Wendy Brown describes as 'a problem of remarks, attitude and speech rather than a matter of historical, political-economic, and cultural formations of power' (Brown, 2001: 35).

We needed to understand the work involved in generating practical solutions to division of perspectives. With no political imagination for alternatives and few political approaches for halting the violence facing black women, especially working-class students, our interpretations hindered us from organizing broadly as 'black students'. Moreover, dogmatic over-reliance on partisan politics, coupled with demarcation through party badges, further alienated non-aligned student activists, workers and allied staff, preventing any wider critique. A culture of anti-intellectualism grew that was intended to undermine the contributions of the 'other' by reinforcing the idea of a split between theory and practice. This produced what bell hooks describes as the denial of liberatory education for critical consciousness (hooks, 1991: 7), contrary to the success of the student-worker dialogues. This argues that the future politics emerging from the student movement(s) must acknowledge the ways in which different groups, especially working class black women and black non-binary people, have been marginalized in even the most progressive spaces.

Lessons for the future

As black women within the student movement and in the eye of the storm, our central concerns were to strengthen the powers of the emancipatory state and consolidate both the monumental and marginal gains, not only in South Africa but for black women across the African Diaspora. Yet I remain concerned about the space within the emerging post-apartheid imagination for the political and intellectual project that many of us had committed our lives to pursuing. The collective histories of political figures, such as Winnie Madikizela Mandela, Hannah Kudjoe, Bibi Titi Mohamed and their colleagues across the continent offered so many inspiring lessons, and they demonstrate the importance of sustaining their political trajectory into the present-past. Our experiences and the failures to address the complex perspectives of a truly intersectional struggle yield important lessons for black women in the UK and elsewhere. This chapter shows that it is crucial to ensure public recognition of black women's contributions to the struggle and their abilities to mobilize and to generate new political and cultural imaginations. We black women activists have a political imperative to eradicate any possibility that our own political intentions and actions are sidelined or footnoted in the archives.

References

Adriaanse, D. (2017) '143 fired UWC guards fight to get jobs back'. *IOL*, 7 March. Online. https://tinyurl.com/uf3zbjm (accessed 8 December 2019).

Allman, J. (2009) 'The disappearing of Hannah Kudjoe: Nationalism, feminism and the tyrannies of history'. *Journal of Women's History*, 21 (3), 13–35.

Biko, S. (1971) 'The definition of black consciousness'. Paper produced for paper produced for a South African Students' Organisation leadership training course in December 1971. Online. https://tinyurl.com/wbwnkow (accessed 30 January 2020).

Biko, S. (1978) *Steve Biko – I Write What I Like: A selection of his writings*. Ed. Stubbs, A. London: Bowerdean Press.

Brown, W. (2001) 'Symptoms: Moralism as anti-politics'. In Brown, W. *Politics out of History*. Princeton: Princeton University Press, 18–44.

Bryan, B., Dadzie, S. and Scafe, S. (1985) *The Heart of the Race: Black women's lives in Britain*. London: Virago.

Bubblegum Club (2016) 'Giving content to decolonisation: The Trans Collective in South Africa'. Online. https://tinyurl.com/sb9oqb9 (accessed 5 May 2018).

Daily Vox (2017) 'Concerned Rhodes academics speak out about #RhodesWar'. 18 December. Online. https://tinyurl.com/u3n4llg (accessed 8 December 2019).

Davis, A.Y. (1981) *Women, Race and Class*. New York: Random House.

Fleischack, A., Macleod, C.I. and Bohmke, W. (2017). '"The man can use that power", "she got courage" and "inimba". Discursive resources in counsellors' talk of intimate partner violence: implication for practice'. *Social Work* 53 (1): 127–44. Online. https://tinyurl.com/y9e8d9vc

Geiger, S. (1997) *TANU Women: Gender and culture in the making of Tanganyikan nationalism, 1955–1965*. Portsmouth, NH: Heinemann.

Gqola, P.D. (2001) 'Contradictory locations: Blackwomen and the discourse of the Black Consciousness Movement (BCM) in South Africa'. *Meridians*, 2 (1), 130–52.

Hassim, S. (2006) *Women's Organizations and Democracy in South Africa: Contesting authority*. Madison: University of Wisconsin Press.

Hill Collins, P. (1990) 'Black feminist thought in the matrix of domination'. In Hill Collins, P. *Black Feminist Thought: Knowledge, consciousness, and the politics of empowerment*. Boston: Unwin Hyman, 221–38.

hooks, b. (1991) 'Theory as liberatory practice'. *Yale Journal of Law and Feminism*, 4 (1), 1–12.

Kamanzi, B. (2016) 'Reflections on "free education" from Sao Paulo to Cape Town – Part 1'. *Daily Maverick*, 12 September. Online. https://tinyurl.com/tn67gs9 (accessed 8 December 2019).

Kelley, R.D.G. (2017) 'What did Cedric Robinson mean by racial capitalism?'. *Boston Review*, 12 January. Online. https://tinyurl.com/lmnbypo (accessed 8 December 2019).

Mangena, M.J.O. (2008) 'The black consciousness philosophy and the woman's question in South Africa: 1970–1980'. In Mngxitama, A., Alexander, A. and Gibson, N.C. (eds) *Biko Lives! Contesting the legacies of Steve Biko*. New York: Palgrave Macmillan, 253–66.

Matandela, M. (2015) 'Rhodes Must Fall: How black women claimed their place'. *Mail and Guardian*, 30 March. Online. https://tinyurl.com/uopyld4 (accessed 8 December 2019).

Mathibela, N. (2017) 'Protest, racism and gender in South Africa'. *Review of African Political Economy*, 9 November. Online. https://tinyurl.com/us8pb97 (accessed 8 December 2019).

Mathibela, N. and Dlakavu, S. (2016) 'Biko lives in fallism'. *News24*, 11 September. Online. www.news24.com/Opinions/biko-lives-in-fallism-20160909 (accessed 1 February 2018).

Mirza, H.S. (2009) *Race, Gender and Educational Desire: Why black women succeed and fail*. London, Routledge.

Motha, S. (2009) 'Archiving colonial sovereignty: From ubuntu to a jurisprudence of sacrifice'. *South African Public Law*, 24 (2), 297–327.

Ndaba, M. (2016) 'Women oppression in FeesMustFall movement'. *MiCampus Magazine*, 4 February. Online. www.micampusmag.co.za/2016/02/secrificing-black-men/ (accessed 28 April 2018).

Ngcobo, L. (1990) *And They Didn't Die*. London: Virago.

Ramose, M.B. (2001) 'An African perspective on justice and race'. *polylog: Forum for Intercultural Philosophy*, 3. Online. http://them.polylog.org/3/frm-en.htm (accessed 8 December 2019).

Ramose, M.B. (2007) 'In memoriam: Sovereignty and the "new" South Africa'. *Griffith Law Review*, 16 (2), 310–29.

Rampele, M. (1990) 'The dynamics of gender within BC Movement in the seventies: Continuities and discontinuities in current liberation movements'. Paper presented at The Legacy of Steven Bantu Biko Seminar, Harare, June 1990.

Rhodes Must Fall (2015) 'UCT Rhodes Must Fall mission statement'. Online. https://tinyurl.com/yx73ybt2 (accessed 8 December 2019).

Seddon, D. (2016) '"We will not be silenced": Rape culture, #RUReferencelist, and the University Currently Known as Rhodes'. *Daily Maverick*, 1 June. Online. https://tinyurl.com/vqnrt68 (accessed 8 December 2019).

Walker, C. (1991) *Women and Resistance in South Africa*. 2nd ed. Cape Town: David Philip Publishers.

Watt, D. and Jones, A.D. (2015) *Catching Hell and Doing Well: Black women in the UK – the Abasindi Cooperative*. London: Trentham Books.

Whiteness in denial: Promoting culturally specific coaching conversations in higher education

Jan Etienne, Jen Davis and Fyna Dowe

> *I began to feel estranged and alienated from the huge group of white women, who were celebrating the power of 'sisterhood'. I could not understand why they did not notice 'absences', or care. When I confronted our teacher, she expressed regret and began to cry. I was not moved, I did not want sympathy, I wanted action. (hooks, 1989:149)*

Introduction

Black students of African heritage are among the fastest growing ethnic groups entering university and face some of the biggest challenges in navigating their way through structural racism in the UK university structure.

In this intergenerational chapter we consider 'Whiteness' in higher education and its impact on black learners. We do so from our perspectives as younger and older multi-faceted activists, social science educators, mentors, entrepreneurs and, in one case, recent re-entrant to higher education. We spell out our intention to support the university in adapting curriculum delivery, challenging static, Eurocentric and outdated models of higher education provision and embracing initiatives that seek ways to inspire and motivate black learners. Our writing is theoretically informed by black feminist epistemology in the work of bell hooks (1989) and relies on our experiences of learning, teaching and activist work in education. In exposing the strength and potential for culturally specific conversations across the curriculum we identify ways to improve black lives in higher education.

The chapter draws on themes raised in earlier chapters in this volume (Chapter 3 and 7 in particular) to demonstrate how it is no longer acceptable in diverse, higher education establishments to ignore the suffering of black students and of black staff. Ultimately we seek to challenge the denial that whiteness impacts negatively on black lives and demonstrate to black students that while structural racism exists, we are determined to play our part in pursuing change in higher education to enable them to reach their potential and achieve academic excellence at the highest levels.

Demanding radical conversations on white privilege

> It is necessary to remember that it is first the potential oppressor within that we must resist – the potential victim within that we must rescue – otherwise we cannot hope for an end to domination, for liberation. (hooks, 1989: 21)

Abysmally low recruitment of senior black academic staff and disproportionately low numbers of black students achieving good grades compared with their white counterparts has created a crisis in British higher education. Until recently, the few black leaders in the UK higher education establishment remained constrained by a misguided loyalty toward their white counterparts who have continued to benefit from the lack of collective black voice on the subject of white privilege in higher education. Such a situation has festered because as black educationalists we have prioritized our professionalism and remained largely passive in an effort to avoid the probable backlash built on the politics of white fear with its deep roots in the radical black power movement in education (Karenga, 1993, Wright, 1984). Such earlier progressive scholars in the US helped pave the way for radical thinking in the UK and have been critical of black academics for their complacency in allowing a Eurocentric environment to flourish in higher education without forceful protest and at the expense of the black learner. Their writings remain absent from the university curriculums, and today while we maintain the need for integrity in ensuring a smooth journey for all our students and ourselves, we recognize the urgency to speak out and confront the challenges we face. We acknowledge that we need to do this not just for our own survival in higher education but for the survival of black learners who depend on us more than ever.

We argue that whiteness in the university is tolerated by black staff, denied by white staff who choose not to discuss it and, according to Rollock (2012), are sometimes oblivious to the extent of their privileges. She points out: '*Whiteness allows White people to proceed in every day practice without recognizing or being conscious of their own racial positioning.*' (Rollock, 2012: 1). Consequently, we have to find ways to convince those who benefit from the invisible hand of whiteness to recognize their privilege and use it to benefit others (Clennon, 2018). In attempting to move forward, Eddo-Lodge points to the impact of discussions of race on the black female:

> Raising racism in a conversation is like flicking a switch. It doesn't matter if it's a person you've just met, or a person you've always felt safe and comfortable with. You're never sure when a conversation about race and racism will turn into one where you were scared for your physical safety or social position. (Eddo-Lodge, 2017: 92)

Inside the university, culturally specific conversations with white staff about white privilege is highly relevant if we are to take collective ownership in tackling racism. How can the issue of supporting black students be taken seriously when we are still defending attacks from our detractors for implementing initiatives aimed at giving young aspiring learners a start in building a stronger foundation for academic success.

Watt and Jones point out:

> The Right argued that black access courses lowered admission standards and the Left was concerned about tokenism and institutionalized marginalization. Some commentators also questioned [about] whether such courses simply added another barrier to black people's entry to higher education and professional careers as some of them led no further. (Watt and Jones, 2015: 153)

We acknowledge the value of such access courses in helping young people progress from secondary education to higher education and for moving second-chance learners (Stevens, 2015) onto degree programmes. For this reason, we support lifelong learning opportunities embedded in higher education introductory studies because they provide an important start in designing support aimed at developing academic writing skills for black learners. However, there is something about the university environment that holds black learners back. And as black women working with younger and older learners in higher education, we are determined to introduce culturally appropriate conversations on ways forward. We seek to share our strategies for achieving academic excellence, and demand radical conversations that are rooted in an urgency to widen black professional involvement and energize black students to evolve from successful achievers into academic role models. We can only do this with the support of our white colleagues, and in a highly competitive research-based university environment we are aware of the many challenges we face.

Whiteness: Acknowledging the challenges and silences in higher education

Currently, the university is facing a backlash for daring to tackle whiteness, decolonize its curriculums (Bhambra *et al.*, 2018; Sabaratnam, 2019) and make it a better, more rewarding place for both black and white students. Whiteness and its generally unacknowledged, normative power continues to be a barrier to change, embedded as it is in the culture of higher education institutions, in racist behaviours, attitudes, emotions, actions and in the thinking of individuals protected by structures and practices that perpetuate systematic racism. Conversations in the media (Quinn, 2011) are influential and debates on measures to decolonize the curriculum rages outside the lecture theatres of higher education (BBC Radio 4, 2019a). Some commentators are offended by blacks who agitate about race, racism and colonialism. What's the problem with the status quo, they ask? Are we implying that well-respected white professors are unsuitable or should not be trusted to lecture on issues such as the ills of imperialism (BBC Radio 4, 2019b)? What about intellectual merit? So called liberal-minded whites are criticized for supporting or putting forward an agenda that is preaching to students rather than allowing them space to discuss and make up their own minds (Phillips, 2019).

According to Bhopal (2018), many of those who are white may not necessarily recognize whiteness or even acknowledge its existence (Bhopal, 2018). Yet, it is problematic to discuss or question ideas when, as blacks, we are inadequately represented in senior roles and our own social research struggles reminds us of what is still missing from the university curriculum. Those who oppose decolonizing the curriculum imply that broadening and diversifying syllabuses will lead to students being taught in dangerous, radical ways. Yet higher education studies involve debate and reasoning. So where is the conversation inside the university?

The reality of whiteness in the university
'Stop blaming it on colonialism'

When black women in higher education speak about our activism, the issues are wide-ranging but we are principally concerned with black youth and combating the effects of whiteness. The social dimension to learning is important to us and we have viewed our predicament from all sides, and now the time is right for us to work closer together with social justice-minded colleagues in a shared strategy for change (Dennis, 2018). In the physical spaces of higher education we are reminded every day that we 'have no history' and therefore no power (this connects with the experiences of transitions in South African universities described in Chapter 9, despite our quite different recent histories). What we may see in the university are token images of ourselves, and as we attempt to progress within it we suffer the trauma of failure and missed opportunities. Some of us have walked these corridors a thousand times but our reflection still evades us – all we feel is the legacy of whiteness and hostility towards us. Who cares about our achievements? Who cares about our contributions? When we discuss our ethnographic research projects as students or researchers we are warned not to blame everything on colonialism. When we ask for suggestions on what we could do to join our higher-ranking white colleagues we are told that we don't mix or network sufficiently with the right people and that we prioritize the wrong missions. We may be offered 'opportunities' that invariably seem as though we're being set up to fail. We learn that we missed out on promotion or funding opportunities because of the fierceness (quality) of the competition. We learn subliminally that we are thought to have neither the intellectual merit nor the cultural capital to rise in this system. Nonetheless, we support our determined white colleagues because everyone has the right to excel if we work hard enough. For some of us, accessing the basic rights to academic success is an uphill struggle but in a new climate of challenging whiteness, all of our voices will be heard.

Whiteness at higher education exam boards

For black female educators in higher education, there are major concerns at undergraduate levels where we are often the only black academic on the internal Exam Board as we listen painfully to overall student results. At times we are working with an all-white female team and feel a sense of alienation. We observe the display board in front of us, year after year, we watch blindly as the individual grades are calculated. We know that the majority of these low grades are being awarded to black students of African Caribbean heritage and know that we can do better by these black students. Compared to their white counterparts, they will not do well at all. The number of re-submissions from black students show that there is little expectation or concern from exam board members at this final stage of the undergraduate journey. The ethnic background of the student cohort will not matter. In some areas, black students will scrape through with a pass, but in many cases we know they deserve much more. While there are moments of elation and pride at undergraduate level when black students are awarded a First, such incidents occur more readily at Master's level when the student is awarded a clear, well-deserved distinction. When black students achieve distinctions at undergraduate level they are awarded because they have a solid track record of strong academic achievement or that they have found some additional support from outside their university. Where black students receive early guidance in a comfortable environment they are on the right path to achieving academic success, and they succeed. A large number of black undergraduate students will require motivation and inspiring role models to achieve the high grades they deserve. A radical university with a strong ethos on close engagement with culturally specific curriculums (Andrews, 2018b) can improve overall achievement and attainment levels of black students.

The academic frustrations of the black undergraduate in higher education

Research detailed in Carnell and Fung (2017) reveals that many black students have reported feeling alienated from the physical and cultural space of the university. Such alienation impacts on their ability to connect at a deep level with what they learn. Based on our own teaching experience in the UK's increasingly diverse university settings, we acknowledge that during the academic year black undergraduate students often share with us a desperate need to be assigned a coach or a mentor, or to have a conversation with a particular black member of staff to discuss their academic progress. While there is much respect for the white academic tutor, there is a burning desire for a face-to-face discussion with a black academic (the next chapter addresses this issue). When discussing research for a project, contact with black academics can make the difference between receiving a pass or a fail or between receiving a first, second or third-class degree. Nonetheless, black students continue to reluctantly accept the Eurocentric nature of the unappealing essay title that does not inspire passion. There is often no enthusiasm to negotiate a question with the course lecturer. The white lecturer cannot always help in inspiring commitment to or motivation for the topic and this is not the fault of the hardworking white lecturer. Motivating and inspiring black students often requires culturally specific interventions in a university structure, particularly where students have to rely on sources of academic references that are, in many places, almost exclusively white. Undergraduate university lectures invariably benefit white students, even when black students are in the majority. White students clearly resonate with the themes, topics and research ideas put across by the authors under study. Shared pedagogical practices when working with diverse students in university settings must be a priority in the struggle to tackle the impacts of whiteness.

There are times when the black student will receive what they consider to be an abrasive, sharp comment from the white lecturer and would search for weeks or months for one-to-one feedback, often to no avail. Students will find that their fellow black student will receive a similarly curt comment from the same lecturer. The white lecturer is evasive when it comes to face-to-face feedback. The student feels he is wasting the lecturer's time and will not persist. The black student is left with a feeling of rejection, and other black students are likely to be feeling the same way. The black student will consider making a complaint to someone but, in an all-white institution, worries about their future or that possible victimization will prevent them from taking further steps. There is no-one to talk to, the personal tutor is absent, the student is told that they are totally booked up; there is no support to be found. As a low-achieving, failing black student, no-one goes out of their way to help. Black students who do not receive positive feedback on meaningful ways to improve course work will remain demotivated and will produce each piece of work just hoping for a pass each time. What's the point of trying to achieve anything more? This situation is unacceptable. Meanwhile the white lecturer is oblivious to the dissatisfaction felt by the black students, and therefore whiteness prevails.

Low recruitment of black academics: 'Impact on the curriculum'

In turning to diversity in delivery of the university curriculum, we recognize the dearth of senior black academics and that appointing more black professors is a necessary part of the solution. Closely related is the fact that teaching black history is highly necessary in delivering enlightening curriculums to all student cohorts. However, our agitators are more likely to argue that if black students are born here they don't need to concern themselves with black history but should concentrate on understanding British culture, values and history. Such individuals conveniently ignore the fact that British colonial history can be seen from diverse perspectives, the harshest of which are often suppressed. Neoliberalism in the university has encouraged individualistic and colour-blind ways of thinking, and proponents of liberal 'free speech' have continued to criticize political correctness in language and actions as political interference, while freedom to criticize society's racism is to be constrained and feared since it represents black extremism. We argue that the elephant in the room is in the strategically placed reference to 'intellectual merit' – used to exclude us while those in positions of power appoint 'on merit' others who look like them and share the same points of cultural reference. Thus, we learn that we may never be good enough, while whiteness in racist institutional structures and practices is ignored. We sit as tokens on interview panels and witness the only black 'would-be academic' being interviewed but who, alas, is told that she lacks sufficient publications or the right kind of publications.

Ignoring whiteness is a major obstacle to progression in the university. We feel the hurt and rage alluded to in an earlier chapter when, in a staff seminar, we are quietly told by a white fellow participant that they are 'afraid to talk about race' on their courses as they 'fear the backlash' of 'getting it wrong'. What of the black student? bell hooks expresses fear and disheartenment as an undergraduate at Stanford University:

> It was disheartening for me and other non-white students to face the extent to which education in the university was not the site of openness and intellectual challenge we had longed for. We hated the racism, the sexism, the domination. I began to have grave doubts about the future. (1989: 100)

Today, as Meghji observes, for black students as well as for black staff, nothing much has changed:

> Racism often means that the racially subordinate must consistently prove that racism exists; we have to constantly defend our experiences from structures and people who downplay the continuing significance of race(ism). (Meghji, 2019: 3)

Post-colonial melancholia and the British university

In discussions on how we can move forward, we stress that the British university has had decades to address issues of structural racism and can be said to be experiencing a type of 'post-colonial melancholia' today. Faced with a moral and radical loss of its legitimacy, it is experiencing a depressed reaction contributing to a 'culture of alienation from and indifference' not only to the past but 'anything that entails responsibility' (Gilroy, 2005). This is indeed worrying since this 'culture of alienation' can allow key players in the university to exist in their segregated, middle class spaces, unburdened by guilt but devoid of ideas and enthusiasm to tackle structural racism as they concentrate on their separate, specialist pursuits, unaware that their disregard for their wider responsibilities impacts negatively on black learners. Senior white staff in the university may silently mourn for empire and what 'they had loved and lost' and the enormity of coping with diverse groups of challenging learners is all too consuming that their collective depression inhibits 'any capacity for responsible or reconstructive practice' (Gilroy, 2004: 107). The university has responsibility and is not exempt from responding to a deplorable legacy of slavery and opening up discussions and confronting the past is no easy task. Gilroy stipulates:

> before the British people can adjust to the horrors of their own modern history and start to build a new national identity from the debris of their broken narcissism, they will have to learn to appreciate the brutalities of colonial rule enacted in their name and to their benefit, to understand the damage it did to their political culture at home and abroad, and to consider the extent of their country's complex investments in the ethnic absolutism that has sustained it. (Gilroy, 2004: 108)

Shirley Ann Tate observes that:

> Whites must avoid the shame of their own racism so racism continues to be melancholically repressed as part of shame's (un)voiceability regime. (Un)voiceability regimes ensure that universities are shorn of any meaningful engagement with race and racism through policies of deracination that make race and racism 'cease to exist'. (Tate, 2017: 62)

Moreover, Shilliam (2018: 59) declares:

> They see the base of the pyramid growing relentlessly blacker, browner, poorer. They seek to preserve the whiteness of elite cultural reproduction in sites that are currently most detached from the pyramid's base. Theirs is a melancholic, reactive mood to an inevitability borne of empire, namely that the fantasy of a pristine West could not hold for too long.

Glasgow University's reparations programme, working with the University of the West Indies, exposes the vast profits it made from African enslavement, and is now proudly working towards restorative justice. Other British universities are slowly following in Glasgow's lead but we must recognize that the actions of white staff matter greatly. Narayan writes of a terror of silence inside academia where 'segregated spaces' exist, and 'where the borders are carefully policed through the cultivation and ferocious protection of silence and the normalization of respectability' (Narayan, 2019). Where silence is protected, the connections between empire and contemporary forms of privilege are hidden by the prevailing air of respectability, and calls for academics to produce material revealing the histories of empire go unheard.

We are committed to finding ways to challenge this terror of silence, and to abolishing contemporary forms of privilege and the normalization of respectability. We believe that our own spaces of recovery and networking remain our vital defence against Whiteness in the university.

Culturally specific coaching conversations in higher education

We propose a two-fold mechanism for acknowledging and combatting whiteness to improve black lives inside the university.

First, a concerted effort to introduce **coaching conversations**, by welcoming a national programme of expert black voices across specialist areas. They would be invited to help deliver key aspects of our higher education curriculums, as specialist guest lectures working in their disciplines, alongside undergraduate teaching staff. This approach is nothing new in higher education; the difference lies in the targeted approach, which complements recruitment strategies designed to increase the number of black professors across the country.

Second, the establishment of a **black campus radio** learning platform to engage in intergenerational dialogue that is dedicated to speaking with black youth on issues related to the higher education curriculum. Such an initiative will involve black learners and black academics from across UK universities working with undergraduates, helping to drive the programme. Such projects will provide spaces for discussions on new research, talks by black experts and PhD students. The initiative will be developed with involvement from the student unions and black women's higher education networks, with the help of black professionals outside the university. The objective is to provide new channels of communication for inspiration aimed at black undergraduates.

The following pages shine a closer light on the need for such developments.

Raising black consciousness in higher education: The introduction of a national higher education coaching strategy

There are growing networks of black educators (Richards, 2017) and black women in higher education across the African diaspora who want to see change in higher education. Some of us were victims of school exclusions, but strong supportive black networks helped us to push through the challenges and support others from wherever we came. As former vice principal of Sir Arthur Lewis College, Agatha Modeste recalled in her interview for the Womanist Black Youth study:

> We reached out to our other mothers and sisters during those early days of struggle and kept in touch. Letter writing was powerful but today, social media platforms help us to strategize – now we need to find ways to widen our dialogue with young people. After black grandmothers worked so hard, their children are killing each other on the streets. (Etienne, 2019)

A culturally specific national coaching strategy in higher education involving black role models can also significantly affect the achievement of undergraduate students. Modelled on the tradition of guest lecturing in social sciences, and with a specific focus on academic writing, black consciousness coaching has the potential to benefit all learners and all staff at undergraduate level. Contractual recruitment of colleagues from other universities and from external bodies to deliver lectures and talks in specialist domains is likely to encourage enthusiasm and focus at critical stages of the student's academic journey. Universities that put aside funding to resource guest lecturing for embedded curriculum coaching initiatives are likely to develop a more successful programme overall, with the potential to narrow the black attainment gap. How can learned black people inside and outside the university work with white academics to recruit senior black academics and diversify the curriculum? We reiterate: universities have failed to close the attainment gap between white students and black, and strategies to decolonize university curriculums are still fiercely criticized by sections of a powerful elite. We call for a national higher education coaching strategy involving black professionals so that we can consolidate our conversations on university curriculums, spread knowledge of the black struggle and improve the academic success rates of black students.

Learning from both black and white staff on ways to navigate against whiteness in the university is paramount in raising the aspirations and attainment of black students. Our discussion groups engage in culturally specific conversations, sharing knowledge. We call for white staff across British universities to understand the need for critical black consciousness to inform higher education curriculums. We seek to expose the structures and practices that hamper the progress of black academics, and to work with existing networks to increase awareness throughout academia.

We aim to combine existing good practice with a targeted strategy to raise black consciousness, involving black professionals from inside and outside the university in seminar discussions funded by the university. We acknowledge the support and willingness for change from notable areas of the higher education sector but also recognize the fear and hopelessness that prevents change in certain areas. Black women's conversations emanate from our diverse experiences when networking across national activist platforms and in the multi-faceted activist roles we occupy. By forging a culturally specific approach, we hope to mitigate the effects of whiteness in the university.

Black faces matter in delivery of the curriculum. We have argued that black learners rarely get taught by people who look like us. The African family and youth aren't reflected positively in society, particularly by the media, and they aren't exposed to consistent culturally specific curriculums backed up with lasting supportive networks. There are few visions of success, and our dreams and aspirations are often stifled at an early age. We consider attainment to be only one side of the coin; the other is character: caring about and contributing to their community and wider society.

Surely, black young people must tire of the same age-old narrative focus on their 'poor education and violence'? Where are the positive stories for black youth? What difference might it make to the quality of their education if they know about black successes, positive black history, their ethnic heritage and roots?

According to Ann Phoenix, black children:

> learn that their parents, and hence they, are excluded from positions of power within society. Black children simultaneously learn that black people are stereotyped in different ways to those by which white people are stereotyped. (Phoenix, 1997: 64)

Today in our research networks, we learn of the significance of education and power. Young black students speak of the loss of their sense of identity, and older learners discuss the hostile environment that kept us silent, becoming victims of the forgotten Windrush generation. Such was this prime example of the impact of exclusion from positions of power where fear allowed for the suppression of our voices. Culturally specific coaching programmes in higher education, be it in science and mathematics, history, philosophy, social sciences, arts or linguistics won't disrupt undergraduate teaching and learning but rather it will enhance academic study (Cole and Heinecke, 2018). In a climate where whiteness dominates, a national and culturally specific coaching programme will be led by black professionals and academics who will deliver lectures to culturally inspire and motivate all groups of undergraduate learners.

Black campus radio: Introducing a new learning platform in our conversation with black youth

Black women are having a new conversation with black youth and they want this to be spread to wider audiences. Black youth have a desire to open up about their frustration and ways in which they can aspire and reach academic heights. We want to learn about the successes and frustrations of young, black people in higher education. We seek to engage with their learning discourse as well as on issues impacting the wider black community. In their networks, young black women are already forging ahead and have developed online radio conversations on lifestyle issues. It is now time for the university to build on this good practice and develop campus learning conversations with black undergraduates. The crisis of black youth has many strands and is rooted in a system of problems, including issues related to education.

We believe that pushing the black brand is a major imperative as our lifestyle choices are in question by a dominantly Eurocentric society. Radio is an important medium to confront issues that are often little understood. In our culturally specific discussions we speak of 'buying black' (products) and promoting natural black hair that to some may appear naïve in a world where freedom and choice are considered the norm. However, 'buying black' is also key to educating black children to be proud of their culture, especially as they are growing up in a society where to be black is often to be left behind on the educational ladder.

Black female and black male role models matter hugely in the lives of black youths but these role models must lead by positive example. It is not just those in the media but also everyday, unseen black men (father activists) going about their lives, working and supporting their communities and families. Engaging in conversations with each other on a national level is paramount, and in that way, we can gain from our collective strengths and understandings.

Kehinde Andrews asserts:

> In terms of producing a radical culture that overcomes the centuries of Western influence, this can only be produced in the furnace of radical action. Communing together, working together and struggling together are the only way to build a society together. (Andrews, 2018a: 175)

Little space exists for black voices to be regularly heard by black people, so connections with the wider African Caribbean diaspora is vital. Black

Campus Learning Radio can be a bridge, and we stress the need for a specific platform for black youth to transmit dialogues for positive change in higher education. Hearing the voices of positive role models and success stories in higher education and opening up discussion on critical themes under the spotlight across university curriculum areas, locally, nationally and internationally. Black youth continue to have major contributions to make and according to Hirsch (2018: 247) 'It's not because black children are less intelligent or capable. Talk to the ones who have proven their potential – against the odds – and this becomes abundantly clear.' Black Campus Radio will prove useful in raising the profile of black learners, involve all generations but will help build a brighter future for a younger generation. The views of black men and the wider black community will help inform and bring communities and generations closer together. Like other communities, the black community is diverse and cuts across, gender, class, sexuality among them, and the views expressed, contributions and intellect will be wide-ranging. Supplementary learning outside the university classrooms and lecture theatres is of vital importance to black students. Akala (2018) stresses the positive impact that Pan African classes had on his life and Adi points that earlier Pan-African conferences 'urged negro intellectuals and all justice-loving men to struggle to create the practical conditions for the revival and growth of Negro cultures (Adi, 2018: 188).

Challenging whiteness and supporting black learners: A way forward

> True politicization – coming to critical consciousness – is a difficult, 'trying' process, one that demands that we give up set ways of thinking and being, that we shift our paradigms, that we open ourselves, to the unknown, the unfamiliar. Undergoing this process we learn what it means to struggle and in this effort we experience the dignity and integrity of being that comes with revolutionary change. (hooks, 1989: 25)

This chapter concludes that whiteness in higher education has much deeper roots in society than in education institutions, and as such, has severe consequences for black staff and black students. Raising aspirations and the academic achievement and attainment levels of black students in higher education demands a collective strategy of culturally specific conversations in the higher education curriculum. Establishing a programme of black lecturers and successful black entrepreneurs, professionals and community activists to coach on undergraduate teaching programmes will require commitment from higher education and a pool of enthusiastic local, regional and international black professionals. Such an initiative is aimed at facilitating greater academic success for black students, just as the presence of black professors in the academy is likely to promote greater confidence and pride, encouraging positive conversations in the higher education academy. An ongoing strategy of coaching conversations with black professionals working alongside undergraduate teaching staff and the additional introduction of a black campus radio initiative to enhance learning and promote active research, will seek to dilute the effects of the denial of the negative impacts of whiteness in higher education. Black women will be at the forefront of such developments as they have consistently been at the sharp end (Amos, 1984; Mirza, 1997) of supporting their communities as tutors, mentors and leaders, inside and outside the academy. bell hooks rightly pointed out that if we do not change our consciousness, we cannot change our actions or demand change for others.

References

Adi, H. (2018) *Pan-Africanism: A history*. London: Bloomsbury Academic.

Akala (2018) *Natives: Race and class in the ruins of empire*. London: Two Roads.

Amos, V. and Parmar, P. (1984) 'Challenging imperial feminism'. *Feminist Review*, 17, 3–19.

Andrews, K. (2016) 'The problem of political blackness: Lessons from the Black Supplementary School Movement'. *Ethnic and Racial Studies*, 39 (11), 2060–78.

Andrews, K. (2018a) *Back to Black: Retelling black radicalism for the 21st Century*. London: Zed Books.

Andrews, K. (2018b) 'The challenge for black studies in the neoliberal university'. In Bhambra, G.K., Gebrial, D. and Nişancıoğlu, K. (eds) *Decolonising the University*. London: Pluto Press, 129–44.

BBC Radio 4 (2019a) '"Decolonising" the curriculum'. *Moral Maze*, 16 February. Online. www.bbc.co.uk/programmes/m0002h1j (accessed 11 December 2019).

BBC Radio 4 (2019b) 'Understanding decolonisation'. *Today* programme, 18 February.

Bhambra, G.K., Nişancıoğlu, K. and Gebrial, D. (eds) (2018) *Decolonising the University*. London: Pluto Press.

Bhopal, K. (2018) *White Privilege: The myth of a post-racial society*. Bristol: Policy Press.

Carnell, B. and Fung, D. (2017) *Developing the Higher Education Curriculum: Research-based education in practice*. London: UCL Press. https://www.uclpress.co.uk/products/95095

Clennon, O.D. (2018) *Black Scholarly Activism between the Academy and Grassroots: A bridge for identities and social justice*. London: Palgrave Pilot. https://tinyurl.com/y7gz3u7c

Cole, R.M. and Heinecke, W.F. (2018) 'Higher education after neoliberalism: Student activism as a guiding light'. *Policy Futures in Education*, 1–27. Online. https://tinyurl.com/s6q2x7h (accessed 10 December 2019).

Dennis, C.A. (2018) 'Decolonising education: A pedagogic intervention'. In Bhambra, G.K., Gebrial, D. and Nişancıoğlu, K. (eds) *Decolonising the University*. London: Pluto Press, 190–207.

Eddo-Lodge, R. (2017) *Why I'm No Longer Talking to White People about Race.* London: Bloomsbury.

Etienne, J (2019) 'Youth crime and violence: Who hears the voices of black women?' Blog post. Online. https://tinyurl.com/vpd8oav (accessed 28 July 2019).

Gilroy, P. (2004) *After Empire: Melancholia or convivial culture?* London: Routledge.

Hirsch, A. (2018) *Brit(ish): On race, identity and belonging.* London: Vintage.

hooks, b. (1989) *Talking Back: Thinking feminist, thinking black.* London: Sheba Feminist Publishers.

Karenga, M. (1993) 'Black psychology'. In Karenga, M. *Introduction to Black Studies*. Los Angeles: University of Sankore Press.

Meghji, A. (2019) 'Contesting racism: How do the black middle-class use cultural consumption for anti-racism?', *Identities*, 1–19. Online. https://doi.org/10.1080/1070289X.2019.1611074

Mirza, H.S. (ed.) (1997) *Black British Feminism: A reader.* London: Routledge.

Narayan, Y. (2019) 'On decolonising our departments and disciplines, respectability and belonging'. Blog post. *Discover Society*, 3 July. Online. https://tinyurl.com/yxk4ylzp (accessed 9 December 2019).

Phillips, M. (2019) 'Decolonising the curriculum is sinister and wrong'. Blog post. Online. https://tinyurl.com/uu6ad6n (accessed 11 December 2019).

Phoenix, A. (1997) 'Theories of gender and black families'. In Mirza, H.S. (ed.) *Black British Feminism: A reader.* London: Routledge, 63–6.

Quinn, B. (2011) 'David Starkey claims "the whites have become black"'. *The Guardian*, 13 August. Online. https://tinyurl.com/ycah6257 (accessed 6 December 2019).

Richards, A. (2017) 'Reclaiming freedom beyond the glass ceiling to transform institutional cultures'. In Gabriel, D. and Tate, S.A. (eds) *Inside the Ivory Tower: Narratives of women of colour surviving and thriving in British academia.* London: Trentham Books, 136–47.

Rollock, N. (2012) 'Unspoken rules of engagement: Navigating racial micro-aggressions in the academic terrain'. *International Journal of Qualitative Studies in Education*, 25 (5), 517–32.

Sabaratnam, M. (2019) 'Postcolonial and decolonial approaches'. In Baylis, J., Smith, S. and Owens, P. (eds) *The Globalization of World Politics: An introduction to international relations*, 160–76. 8th ed. Oxford: Oxford University Press.

Shilliam, R. (2018) 'Black/academia'. In Bhambra, G.K., Gebrial, D. and Nişancıoğlu, K. (eds) *Decolonising the University*. London: Pluto Press, 53–63.

Stevens, P. (2015) *Rita and Gerald: Adult learning in Britain today.* London: Trentham Books.

Tate, S.A. (2017) 'How do you feel? "Well-being" as a deracinated strategic goal in UK universities'. In Gabriel, D. and Tate, S.A. (eds) *Inside the Ivory Tower: Narratives of women of colour surviving and thriving in British academia.* London: Trentham Books, 54–66.

Universities UK and NUS (National Union of Students) (2019) *Black, Asian and Minority Ethnic Student Attainment at UK Universities: #ClosingtheGap.* London: Universities UK and National Union of Students.

Watt, D. and Jones, A.D. (2015) *Catching Hell and Doing Well: Black women in the UK – the Abasindi Cooperative.* London: Trentham Books.

Wright, B.E. (1984) *The Psychopathic Racial Personality, and other essays.* Chicago: Third World Press.

Chapter 11

Supporting black sisters in UK higher education: A question of activism

Uvanney Maylor

Introduction

This chapter seeks to expose challenges faced by Black woman academics and black female students in English higher education, and to show how we might use such difficulties to promote community activism. It stems from my experiences of supporting students at masters and doctoral level to overcome challenges that could undermine their commitment to succeed in higher education. These challenges relate to questions about their ability and what they perceive as lack of understanding by white academics when they choose to study topics that are black-focused or have race as a central dimension so are deemed 'not academic or worthy of study'. Over the years I have received numerous words of appreciation from black students, and this leads me to examine my strategies for supporting them and the extent to which institutional expectations pose challenges.

Utilizing a Black feminist (Hill Collins, 2000; Richards, 2013) and Womanist (Walker, 1983) lens, along with theories associated with an 'ethic of care', the chapter describes my engagement with Black community activism in areas of health, education and politics, and how such engagement provided the basis from which I garner strength from Black women academics and their solidarity, and in turn I feel empowered to support Black women students. Arguably, such support comes at a cost as Black female academics are underrepresented in English higher education (ECU, 2011; HESA, 2018), which means a small number of us are increasingly called on to advocate for and support Black students, potentially overstretching and weakening us. The chapter reveals resistance and survival skills (Lomax, 2015) developed along the way to support Black women students as they navigate higher education. It concludes by highlighting strategies to promote effective and much-needed educational community activism.

Understanding teaching and the significance of racial and cultural background

I am a Black (African-Caribbean) feminist academic working in English higher education in a post-1992 university, an institution associated with widening participation, which encourages students who might not ordinarily have considered studying at university to undertake degree study. My job title is Professor of Education, though I define myself as a sociologist. My research interests include race, ethnicity, culture, educational equity, inclusion and social justice. These interests are all largely informed by a wider concern about the impact of race and culture on educational practice and leadership, and on Black student and teacher experience, identities and outcomes. My aim is to understand how the ethnic/racial/cultural background of teachers and lecturers influences the way they teach students who share or don't share their background, and how the students' identity influences their academic attainment. My concern is partly informed by the persistent lower attainment of Black (African-Caribbean) learners in national examinations at age 16 and in higher education (HESA, 2018). Redressing the imbalance is my reason for working in higher education. To explain my commitment and role vis-à-vis Black female students, I will first share how I arrived in academia.

The roots of my activism and Womanist ideals

Following completion of my doctorate and prior to working in higher education, I sought to understand my true 'self', a self that I had yet to define. During my quest for self-understanding I had three community engagement roles: awareness and development officer (for a cancer charity), research and development officer (for a Black community organization) and volunteer for a Black sickle cell charity. The purpose of the awareness-raising role was to create a culture of learning about breast cancer and a change in health screening behaviour. Through that role I encountered Black and minority ethnic women of mature age with ample life experience, but little knowledge about breast cancer and the implications for their health. For many, cancer was a taboo subject. These women also had little experience of working with someone they considered young enough to be their daughter (and in some cases granddaughter), and whom they expected should listen rather than give advice or try to engage them in training. From these women I learnt that sharing gender and ethnicity and creating safe community spaces wasn't enough to engage in productive dialogue or to secure their participation. What they required was an awareness of their

Womanist ideals and my willingness to understanding them as individuals and how they lived and interacted with their families, wider communities and societal structures and institutions. Essentially, they wanted me to listen and hear their voices, and I learned from Alice Walker (1983) that understanding a woman's voice is crucial to understanding her inner self (such understanding is also essential for Black educators if they are to teach their students how to challenge the status quo. Through working together, we built a learning community (Etienne, 2016) in which we all believed in the others, looked out for each other, tackled difficulties and shared in the highs and lows (vis-à-vis family and health) together. That sense of community still underpins my way of being today.

A key aspect of my research and development role was to examine young black males' perceptions and experiences of crime. I undertook this challenge at a time when Black parents were trying to get justice for Black deaths in police custody and trying to prevent their sons from being criminalized as 'muggers' by trying to overturn the stereotyped perceptions of Black men. Sadly, such perceptions remain entrenched in the UK (Lammy, 2017) and the US. I attended several town hall meetings and observed black parents and the wider black community come together despite police intimidation (such as being monitored by CCTV, encountering police in riot gear) and the threat to their liberty, to demand answers and challenge the deaths in police custody. In those meetings I saw how parents (often strangers to each other) drew strength from one another and used it to fuel their community activism by, for instance, organizing meetings with the leader of the Greater London Authority and the Metropolitan Police Commissioner). I always left those meetings with a sense of pride, feeling stronger, empowered and wanting to make a difference to Black lives through community activism and advocating for those unable to do so for themselves.

I was at the same time working as a volunteer at a sickle cell charity, advocating on behalf of sickle cell sufferers, and challenging the perceptions the ambulance service and health authority held of sickle cell sufferers – that they were drug addicts because of how they looked when experiencing a pain crisis.

Through these varied roles I committed myself to serving the Black community, embodying the values of care and providing Black-on-Black support wherever possible. However, it was when I re-entered higher education that I fully understood the roots of my community activism: Black feminism and Womanist ideals.

Theoretical framework for exploring an ethic of care

The rest of this chapter content is theorized using Black feminist and Womanist ideologies as propounded by Hill Collins (2000), Walker (1983) and Etienne (2016). A key aspect of Black feminist perspectives relating to the role of Black women is the role of mothers. 'Mothering' (Foster, 1993) is expected to be delivered with an 'ethic of care', which Collins defines as 'where Black women feel accountable to all the Black community's children [regarding] them as if they were members of their own families' (Collins, 1987: 5, cited by James, 1993: 47). As the definition suggests, an ethic of care is not just applied by a mother to her own children but to all Black children within her community. In this respect an 'ethic of care' is known as 'other/community' mothering.

However, it would be wrong to view 'other mothers' as merely mothering other people's children. The role is a community role, applied to adults and children alike. An 'other mother' is able to apply an ethic of care to the community beyond her immediate family because on the one hand, she commands respect within her community as an older woman, and, on the other, she has knowledge of her community that enables her to 'analyse and/or critique situations that may affect the well-being of her community' (James, 1993: 48). An 'other mother' also 'serves as a catalyst in the development and implementation of strategies designed to remedy these harmful conditions' (James, 1993: 48), consequently an ethic of care is crucial to 'the survival and well-being of the Black community' (James, 1993). Importantly, community 'other mothering' demands a political commitment, which Anim-Addo (2014: 44) describes as:

> a politics of potential, pluralistic and democratic community building, where Black thought and everyday living carry a primary and participant role. The personal – mothering our children – is the political, affording nurturing of alterity through a politics of care that is fundamentally anti-racist and antisexist.

Other mothering through a politics of care is also necessary in higher education because 'young Black people living in a hostile, racist society find themselves too often separated from guidance imbued with care' (Anim-Addo, 2014: 58). This 'politics of care' is what underpins Anim-Addo's (2014) feminist interventions in higher education, which are informed by her 'own difficult experience with higher education' (ibid.: 48) and her understanding of the difficulties encountered by other Black women.

Like an 'other mother', a 'Womanist' is typified through the strengthening and survival role that she plays with regard to Black women (Moultrie, 2017). Walker (1983) considers a Womanist to be a responsible Black woman who loves and is committed to the well-being of other women. A Womanist values and nurtures the Black woman's strength while trying to understand their emotional needs and how best to support them.

It is the combination of my community ethic of care and my feminist Womanist political commitment to do my best to support Black women students in higher education that I explore here; a commitment inspired by my community activism.

Black academic representation in English higher education and student representation and support

Black women students have a higher representation than black men in English higher education (HEFCE, 2017) but, like Black men, their representation does not necessarily translate into good degree outcomes (HESA, 2018). When faced with Black university students an ever-present concern among Black academics is that undergraduate level national degree awards consistently show that these students attain lower grades than white students (Connor *et al.*, 2004; Leslie, 2005; ECU, 2008; Richardson, 2015). Therefore, at postgraduate level it is imperative that stereotyped perceptions of the potential of Black students do not become a self-fulfilling prophecy. But for black academics to effect change is challenging as they are markedly under-represented in English higher education institutions (ECU and HEA, 2008).

Circumventing Black student failure: A social responsibility

In line with my commitment to an ethic of care, I, like Moore (2017: 202), consider supporting and mentoring Black students to be 'a social responsibility'. In fulfilling this, Moore observes that Black women academics who seek to assume this 'responsibility' will find that they occupy a contradictory position of privilege (having power by virtue of their employment in the academy) and marginalization (owing partly to being so under-represented). Moore observes that:

> The service that women of colour are consistently asked to perform, and sometimes feel a personal obligation to participate in, tends to go unreported and unacknowledged, many times even by the individuals doing the work. (Moore, 2017: 200)

Although I acknowledge the double-edged racialized and gendered position Black women academics find themselves in, I am less concerned about the lack of institutional recognition and reward experienced by those who undertake such roles. The rewards come from the Black women students who thank us enthusiastically for helping them so much (see below). What matters most is that Black students receive sensitive and specifically tailored support so that they succeed in their studies. Meeting students' individual needs is time-consuming and demands far more time than is usually allocated as part of their workload. So instead of addressing all the required areas, tutors may only be able to provide an overview of the areas that need addressing. My undergraduate students inevitably raise this on course validation panels I sit on in my own institution and as an external panel member in others. This issue also arises at postgraduate level, sometimes from students who are not my own students. Their comments seem to be saying that my white colleagues don't provide the same level of support as I try to do, as we see from this postgraduate student, who wrote to me in May 2018:

> Hi Uvanney,
>
> Thank you. The comments were so detailed and helpful ... I am so grateful for the level of thought you have given this. My [white] supervisors saw an earlier draft and did not pick up on any of the things you have mentioned so I am truly grateful ...

I am not suggesting that white academics don't provide detailed feedback, but rather that the Black women students who have sought my help are complaining about not experiencing such support from the white academics responsible for marking their work. The frequency of such complaints leads me to believe that there is cause for concern. Academics, both Black and white, need to understand the whole student experience, including issues in their lives that may affect their studies. The apparent lack of understanding of the experiences of Black students in higher education and the effects of racism, and the poor understanding of the racialized topics many choose to study, cause constant concern. One Black doctoral student's experience is a case in point: she specifically requested that I join her doctoral supervisory team after I had reviewed her work as part of an upgrade process.

Given Black students' experiences of racism in universities (Housee, 2018), providing sensitive support to Black students is a social responsibility that falls to Black academics. It is this small cohort who will enable Black students to challenge racist experiences so they can survive in higher education.

However, at times it is the very students I am trying to support who find themselves categorized as 'angry' that consider my support to be insufficient and I face a backlash. For example, one Black woman studying for a doctorate informed me that I was only 70 per cent supportive of her, despite the interventions I had sent via email, the phone calls I made, meetings I attended to advocate on her behalf and the detailed feedback I gave on her work. When I asked what would earn me the further 30 per cent, she said she 'had yet to decide'. Have higher education institutions any idea of the extent of the additional pressures Black academics face? I can only take comfort from the many other Black women students in HE institutions who have contacted me for help on the recommendation of others.

White and Black staff sharing their experiences

Recently, a white academic told me she was anxious that a Black female doctoral student whom we both supervised was more likely to come to me than to her for support and that she didn't understand why. I found myself explaining that the student had contacted me for support outside office hours and had talked to me at length about the racism she had encountered from a member of staff. She told me she urgently needed to share the experience with someone whom she believed would understand and not think she was 'overreacting'. After I told the white staff member this, she concluded that the reason the student didn't come directly to her could be that the student saw her as 'part of the problem'. In contrast to the Black academics, the white staff member focused on herself rather than on the student's feelings and experience, whereas sharing her experience with me enabled the student to express her frustration about the racist experience and then to listen to my suggested strategies for addressing the matter.

Strategies employed to support Black women students and staff

Henry (1992) associates the caring exhibited by Black teachers with resistance, while for Siddle Walker (1996: 3) Black teachers combine caring, 'support [and] encouragement' with 'rigid [academic] standards'; they take a 'personal interest' in their students and try to 'not let them go wrong'. In my view, this is the difference a politics of care makes to the nature and level of support Black women students require. While I support all my students, the support I offer Black women postgraduate students is a mixture of that articulated by Henry and Walker, who encourages teachers to help students manifest their 'voice' and 'make them [feel] visible, significant, important, and centred rather than marginalized, ignored, and unnoticed'. To such support I add an 'ethic of care' (Richards, 2013) so that the support benefits the students concerned. My strategies operate across five distinct lines:

First, as a result of my activist education experience, I regard myself as a natural nurturer of Black women's academic abilities – encouraging them to recognize their talent and cherishing them so they feel able to show their capabilities. Second, I feel able to give them the confidence to articulate their views, realize their resilience and take the (resistant) actions needed, equipping them with new tools to write their assignments and making changes to their studies. Third, my goal is to ensure that they understand their entitlement to social justice in their education. Fourth, I believe I have a duty to serve, and in line with Moore's concept of 'social responsibility', the support I offer Black women is to enable them to enhance their studies and their lives, rather than enjoying any benefit I might derive from their degree awards. Fifth, something I do unreservedly is become an emotional crutch in the women's hour of need, usually in my own time, when they know I will give my undivided attention to listen to their problems such as worry about assignment grades, course registration anomalies, lack of access to library resources or payment of fees. These women know that they can share study and home-related anxieties and worries with me as their supervisor, and that I will do my best to help and provide the sensitive, tailored support they require. The resistant support (Wright *et al.*, 2018) I provide sometimes makes me a buffer between my students and white academic power structures (Moore, 2017) where we're perceived as 'Angry Black Women'.

Support for the Black woman academic

As the sole Black female academic in a senior position in my institution, I also play an important role in supporting the Black women working in non-academic roles. A Black member of staff I once met briefly emailed me asking to discuss an urgent issue. We met over coffee to discuss racism from a white member of staff with whom she shared an office. The situation was affecting my colleague's well-being and needed to be dealt with. The following week I received an email from her early one morning followed by an urgent phone call. By 8.15am we had a plan of action, which we executed by 9.15am. When the white staff member arrived at work, her Black colleague told her why she considered her actions to be racist and the impact this had had on her, so that things needed to change. When I followed up with my Black colleague, she reassured me, saying that she had felt emboldened by making her roommate aware of why her actions had been problematic, and that she was certain things would change.

The urgency to support the wider Black community

Supporting all my students matters to me, and supporting the Black women students is essential. These women are often called upon to support members of the wider Black community, especially when there is an impending or sudden death in the community. In addition, they are not cocooned from the realities of everyday racism (Essed, 1991), such as a death in police custody or a young person losing their life at the hands of another while they pursue their studies (such cases can take a year to come to trial). These are real examples of what can happen at any point, and the student may well be devastated and find it impossible to concentrate or study. She may fail assignments in contrast to producing excellent work previously. If we need more evidence of the debilitating effects of life-changing news, we need only see what happened to Serena Williams, holder of 23 Open tennis titles. After hearing that the man who had murdered her sister had been released from prison early, Williams produced the worst result of her tennis career. A week later, she lost the Wimbledon women's 2018 tennis final to a player she might well have beaten on a normal day (*Guardian Sport*, 2018).

My experience in supporting Black women in higher education has made it clear that even if their immediate family is not finding life difficult, they are invariably juggling their studies while trying to support community members at times of crisis, for instance people in poor health or facing terminal illness, or being made redundant. Thus, these students are not just trying to gain a degree or higher degree but have personal concerns too. As an 'other mother' I'm entrusted with knowledge of such crises and 'burdens' that are not brought to the door of white academics, male or female, who do not share their racialized and gendered position.

Many of the Black women students I have encountered are from working-class backgrounds. As such, they come up at times against institutional structures that advocate wider participation and encourage working class participation but in practice cannot accommodate students who lack economic security. Universities are essentially white, middle class institutions, and this accentuates Black women's class differences.

They are also subject to demands from their community: these students expect Black academics to view their study and assignments as a shared community concern. This is why Black female students need and demand racialized and gendered community support from Black women academics. This is another pressure not experienced by white academics.

Despite some shared experiences of gender, white colleagues don't share the same racialized community expectations, nor do they have personal investment in individual Black female students completing their courses successfully. Each Black female success is one step closer to uplifting the community, and it is Black women who largely bear the responsibility for educating Black children (their own and others') and grandchildren (Hill Collins, 2000; Etienne, 2016).

Conclusion

As a community activist and a strong believer in the ethics and politics of care enacted by Black women, I have offered examples of my helping Black female students to illustrate how we Black sisters in academia can lighten their burdens and improve their chances of success. Caring and supporting students to help themselves is an act of resistance and can promote wider change in the long term. At times Black students find themselves taken down a path by a white supervising academic who totally misunderstands why their work has a racial focus, or assesses their work poorly. We must redress these inadequate understandings and ensure that students are given the critical feedback they need to improve and successfully complete their studies.

Receiving support of this kind is key to students learning to help themselves and become community activists. Once their eyes are open to the injustices students may encounter in higher education, they are able to help others. Although Black female students do need particular care and attention, Anim-Addo (2014: 48) has questioned 'the viability of (other) mothering of the mind of [students in higher education when] seasoned Black feminists are suffering "burn-out" or fatigue'. I do not deny that community support and 'other mothering' can be tiring and consuming but I wish to end by stating that the happiest times of my life in academia have been when I have witnessed Black women students who were earmarked for failure or discarded as being unable to make the grade, go on to graduate with honours or receive their doctorates. These successes constitute small but important acts of resistance.

References

Anim-Addo, J. (2014) 'Activist-mothers maybe, sisters surely? Black British feminism, absence and transformation'. *Feminist Review*, 108, 44–60.

Connor, H., Tyers, C., Modood, T. and Hillage, J. (2004) *Why the Difference? A closer look at higher education minority ethnic students and graduates* (Research Report 552). Nottingham: Department for Education and Skills.

ECU (Equality Challenge Unit) (2011) *The Experience of Black and Minority Ethnic Staff in Higher Education in England*. London: Equality Challenge Unit.

ECU (Equality Challenge Unit) and HEA (Higher Education Academy) (2008) *Ethnicity, Gender and Degree Attainment Project: Final report*. York: Higher Education Academy.

Essed, P. (1991) *Understanding Everyday Racism: An Interdisciplinary Theory*. Newbury Park: Sage.

Etienne, J. (2016) *Learning in Womanist Ways: Narratives of first-generation African Caribbean women*. London: Trentham Books.

Foster, M. (1993) 'Othermothers: Exploring the educational philosophy of black American women teachers'. In Arnot, M. and Weiler, K. (eds) *Feminism and Social Justice in Education: International perspectives*. London: Falmer Press, 101–23.

Foster, M. (1997) *Black Teachers on Teaching*. New York: New Press.

Gillborn, D. (2008) *Racism and Education: Coincidence or conspiracy?* London: Routledge.

Guardian Sport (2018) 'Johanna Konta inflicts heaviest defeat of Serena Williams's career'. *The Guardian*, 1 August. Online. https://tinyurl.com/ya3esngl (accessed 6 December 2019).

HEFCE (Higher Education Funding Council for England) (2017) 'Student characteristics'. Online. https://tinyurl.com/tb8kuyb (accessed 11 December 2019).

Henry, A. (1992) 'African Canadian women teachers' activism: Recreating communities of caring and resistance'. *Journal of Negro Education*, 61 (3), 392–404.

HESA (Higher Education Statistics Agency) (2018) 'Higher Education Staff Statistics: UK, 2016/17'. Online. www.hesa.ac.uk/news/18-01-2018/sfr248-higher-education-staff-statistics (accessed 28 April 2020).

Hill Collins, P. (2000) *Black Feminist Thought: Knowledge, consciousness, and the politics of empowerment*. 2nd ed. New York: Routledge.

Housee, S. (2018) *Speaking Out against Racism in the University Space*. London: UCL IOE Press.

James, S.M. (1993) 'Mothering: A possible black feminist link to social transformation?'. In James, S.M. and Busia, A.P.A. (eds) *Theorizing Black Feminisms: The visionary pragmatism of black women*. London: Routledge, 44–54.

Lammy, D. (2017) *The Lammy Review: An independent review into the treatment of, and outcomes for, black, Asian and minority ethnic individuals in the criminal justice system*. London: Lammy Review. Online. https://tinyurl.com/yyctz8zf (accessed 9 December 2019).

Leslie, D. (2005) 'Why people from the UK's minority ethnic communities achieve weaker degree results than whites'. *Applied Economics*, 37 (6), 619–32.

Lomax, T. (2015) 'Black women's lives don't matter in academia either, or why I quit academic spaces that don't value black women's life and labor'. *Feminist Wire*, 18 May. Online. https://tinyurl.com/wo7fhsr (accessed 11 December 2019).

Moore, M.R. (2017) 'Women of color in the academy: Navigating multiple intersections and multiple hierarchies'. *Social Problems*, 64 (2), 200–5.

Moultrie, M. (2017) *Passionate and Pious: Religious media and black women's sexuality*. Durham, NC: Duke University Press.

Richards, D.A.J. (2013) *Resisting Injustice and the Feminist Ethics of Care in the Age of Obama*. New York: Routledge.

Richardson, J.T.E. (2015) 'The under-attainment of ethnic minority students in UK higher education: What we know and what we don't know'. *Journal of Further and Higher Education*, 39 (2), 278–91.

Siddle Walker, V. (1996) *Their Highest Potential: An African-American school community in the segregated South*. Chapel Hill: University of North Carolina Press.

Walker, A. (1983) *In Search of Our Mothers' Gardens: Womanist prose*. San Diego: Harcourt Brace Jovanovich.

Wright, C., Maylor, U. and Watson, V. (2018) 'Black women academics and senior managers resisting gendered racism in British higher education institutions'. In Perlow, O.N., Wheeler, D.I., Bethea, S.L. and Scott, B.M. (eds) *Black Women's Liberatory Pedagogies: Resistance, transformation, and healing within and beyond the academy*. Cham: Palgrave Macmillan, 65–83.

Beyond Brexit: Black women in higher education collaborating internationally for change

Jan Etienne

Black lives are at risk from the onslaught by the rising neofascist and xenophobic groups across much of Europe. It has never been more urgent that the voices of black women in education be heard.

Black women occupy a variety of spaces across the African diaspora and many of us feel uneasy about putting our education ahead of supporting the wider black family. Amid chaotic politics and crises triggered by socio-economic austerity and the resulting populist and racist movements that cast blame on the 'other', we have to make up for lost time and combine our education with our activism. The valuable thinking around black supplementary schools of the 1980s (see Bryan *et al.*, 1985) is as relevant today as it has ever been, and the renewed support for the principles of Pan-Africanism inspires our educational and activist journeys. We are confronting the roots of racism in the white institution, researching and tackling school exclusions, comparing educational opportunities and attainment, and calling for greater representation of black professors inside the British university. Black women's activism matters, and in joining campaigns to decolonize the curriculum and university culture we have become part of a united struggle to tackle the major social crisis in black communities.

The contributors to this book have pointed to 'the discriminatory and exclusionary practices in UK universities that stifle creativity, hinder effective participation in knowledge production, block professional progression and legitimate white supremacy in academia'. They have indicated the similar barriers to achievement in Britain's schools, and the pejorative labelling that has undermined the identities of many young black people who may then seek status elsewhere, sometimes in criminal activity. Despite the hurdles we and our community-based sisters face, we black women academics have a unique opportunity to change the discourse and agenda of research on black communities to an agenda that will transform young people's outcomes.

We acknowledge that the modern university cannot be radically transformed by merely adding darker faces, safer spaces, better training, and a curriculum that acknowledges historical and contemporary oppressions. We need to look beyond the modern university, to find collaborative emancipatory spaces of activism. We can envisage our academic labour as resistance – as the preceding chapters show – be it through diversifying the curriculum, supporting student movements or embracing research projects aimed directly at revealing and tackling social injustice.

As our appreciation of our collective and often hidden individual activism develops, we consider the role education has played in freeing our minds and helping us play our part in the creation of a better world. As the crisis of social conflict that affects the lives of British black – and especially black youth – deepens, our collaborative activism matters most of all.

We must take care not to be complicit in the oppression of black people by doing slave labour – i.e. addressing the topics and the research questions that serve our oppressors' interests. We might be rewarded for it, but too often we become the black silent assistant/collaborator/partner: the euphemism that is used to justify the unequal relationship has just become more sophisticated. We may side with other oppressed groups, but we frequently find ourselves fighting battles on our own.

Thinking in Womanist or intersectional ways allows us to produce knowledge that speaks to the lived experiences of our communities and of the international black world, as we endure common experiences of white privilege and racism.

Having suffered alienating learning environments ourselves, we should use what little power we have to enable a more supportive environment for today's students. Some critics have argued that wanting safe spaces, religious spaces and psychological support may help individual students deal with everyday micro-aggressions and are easy concessions for universities to grant because they don't challenge the structure of the university itself. These safe spaces are still critical to black staff survival and black students' well-being. We must hope that from them, dialogue and resistance can be built.

Together we discussed how we could build a learning community in which we all believe: where we look out for each other, tackle difficulties and create that sense of community that still underpins our way of being. We played a role when black parents were trying to get justice for their children's deaths in police custody, and we played another role to challenge stereotyped perceptions of black men and thus prevent their sons from being criminalized as 'muggers'. We left those meetings and campaigns with a sense of pride, feeling empowered to make a difference to black lives through community activism and by advocating for those unable to do so for themselves.

One of our abiding concerns is the lack of understanding by the academy of the experiences of black students: its micro-aggressions and racism, its devaluing of their academic abilities, and its failure to understand why black students often choose racialized topics to study. In carrying out our research and writing these chapters, we have found it impossible not to revisit our own experiences as black school pupils and university students.

Moreover, while pursuing our studies we too are not cocooned from the realities of everyday racism, such as a death in police custody or when a young life is lost at the hands of another. Such cases can take a year or more before they come to trial and they are all too close to us. Cases that we've identified in the book are real examples. Something like that can happen at any point in a student's studies or among our own friends and communities.

Since the ethnic monitoring of educational outcomes commenced, research has shown that differences in achievement between ethnic groups cannot be explained solely by socio-economic class, and subsequent studies have identified a range of ways in which black pupils and students have been poorly served by the British education system.

In this volume, we call for the establishment of 'a Womanist Forum' as part of a renewed and better-resourced Black Voluntary Sector, to work with schools and other agencies. Black women have an important role in raising and supporting our young people's aspiration.

We demonstrate how our social media blogs promote and become part of our activist conversations. Some of us have been inspired by young black female writers and activists who write how they feel, letting the words speak for themselves. Words are small contributions to our wider narrative – playing a part in protest on deeply challenging issues. Throughout the volume we share the challenges across the social and generational divides, and we illustrate our contributions as black women working with others in education and other projects to tackle structural racism and other forms of social injustice as they impact on black lives.

We note that all over the world black voices are largely suppressed when they speak about tackling critical issues such as black youth violence. Across the African diaspora black women's activism has historically been obscured rather than made clearly visible in male-dominated literary communities, policy formation and liberation history. We seek to dismantle the overwhelming whiteness that pervades our areas of activist work. Our research and activism continues to be for social justice, and is fired by a determination borne out of our personal struggle. Accordingly, we call for a national coaching strategy in higher education, to enable black academics across the country and internationally to work collegially alongside the higher education institutions at undergraduate levels, to support higher education staff and inspire all learners.

As I write this final chapter, the long-awaited Brexit debate appears to be reaching a climax, in the hands of a recently appointed leader of the British government who is willing to defy democratic institutions. Major funding has purportedly been earmarked for education and the police service. Stop and search powers, however, are at their highest levels yet. Political promises are plentiful but there are few signs of any political will to tackle the issues raised in this book. Black women are rising to face the challenges now, and those yet to come.

Empty promises is what people hear
Government cuts each and every year
Cupboards open, bare and scanty
Children in social housing livin in shanty
Forced to play on de pavement
No hope of future employment
Each week mudder playing de Euro millions lotto
Trying anyting to escape from de ghetto

We are not a forgotten race
Let we stand together, mek a difference in dis here place
De vulnerable youth we must embrace
Support one another, be a united force
An' swerve deh life from dis wretched course

Extract from 'De Juk' by Tanty Mauvais
(learninginwomanistways.com, 2019)

Reference

Bryan, B., Dadzie, S. and Scafe, S. (1985) *The Heart of the Race: Black women's lives in Britain*. London: Virago.

Index

Index